MAKING YOUR OWN BABY FOOD

MAKING YOUR OWN BABY FOOD

MARY DUSTAN TURNER
AND
JAMES S. TURNER

REVISED, UPDATED
AND EXPANDED EDITION

WORKMAN
PUBLISHING COMPANY,
NEW YORK

Library of Congress Cataloging in Publication Data

Turner, Mary Dustan.
  Making your own baby food.

  Bibliography: p.
  Includes index.
  1. Infants—Nutrition.   2. Cookery (Baby foods)
I. Turner, James S., joint author.   II. Title.
RJ216.T79   1976   649'.3   76-25808
ISBN 0-911104-89-5
ISBN 0-911104-90-9 pbk.

Workman Publishing Company, Inc.
231 East 51 Street
New York, New York 10022

Book Design: Paul Hanson
Jacket Design: Paul Hanson
Jacket Photograph: Kathryn Abbe
Manufactured in the United States of America

First Printing, January 1977
1 3 5 7 9 8 6 4 2

For our grandmother, Margaret Stocke Hauser, who made it all possible, and

Our dear friend Louanne Bushong Weissberg who supported our efforts and provided many recipes.

This book is the result of our own concern but it could not possibly have been written without the active interest and practical contributions of: Janie Albro, Beth Daniels, Leah Dreger, Mary Dustan, Phillip Dustan, Alys Hale, Mary Karassik, Ruth Kirtland, Tillie Kornfeld, Judy Lang, Patricia Moots, Jane Morton, Carol Richardson, Christopher B. Turner, Edna Weissberg and Sandra Wiener.

CONTENTS

PART IV: THE APPENDIXES

INTRODUCTION

Our interest in the nature of the food supply began in 1965 when our son was a little more than seven months away from being born. At that time Mary—as a result of consultation with her physician—began to carefully assess the food she ate and influenced Jim to begin doing the same. As a result, habits which had been a part of our lives for as long as we could remember began to change noticeably. For example, the two or three soft drinks a day which Jim had consumed for years disappeared from the menu. We learned that counting calories without counting nutrients can be dangerous business. We learned the nutritional reason why good hard-crusted whole-wheat bread is preferred to its white cousins. We asked ourselves how we could avoid the increasing difficulties presented by the processed food supply while we maintained some semblance of sanity and decided that perhaps by raising questions about baby food, we could balance the claims of those who argue there is nothing good about American food against those who argue that everything is good about the American food supply.

When a baby is about to be born, all attention turns, naturally, to its well-being. There is no better time to assess the strengths and weaknesses in its nutritional environment. That nutritional environment might well have as much, if not more, to do with the well-being of the individual infant than any of the thousands of national and international events about which each individual in this society is so constantly and insistently informed.

Until recently, even the most concerned parents took babyfeeding largely for granted. Unless there were special problems, parents assumed that the processed baby foods they bought were generally safe and nutritious. For the most part, little authoritative information was available on infants' individual food needs, proper feeding patterns for each stage of their development, dietary requirements for expectant mothers and other important aspects of the nutritional environment.

Today, people are becoming more and more skeptical about the quality of the food they buy—not only for infants, but for the entire family.

The emphasis from the commercial baby food companies, and from many doctors, unfortunately, is on the necessity of introducing an infant to a wide variety of taste experiences. This has magnified the business of feeding out of all proportion to what is healthy or what is psychologically valuable for the baby. Certainly this has made more work and anxiety for parents. Prior to the industry's development, babies were nursed until two years of age and older. They were fed mashed up foods from their mothers' plates when they could sit up and express interest in solid foods. Parents never made a fuss about when to introduce fruit, meat or cereal. They let the baby decide. Now many parents are returning to that system.

Over the last few years when talking to the many parents who contacted us, we discovered that since we wrote the first edition of *Making Your Own Baby Food* in 1971–72, many more are in fact making their own baby food. The majority of parents make very simple fresh foods for the rest of their families and put the baby's portion in the blender without any seasoning or fussing. They are so confident that they are providing better nutrition for their baby that it is no longer necessary to think or talk about it. If both parents are to find time to hold jobs or develop their special talents, they can not be swamped with anxieties about whether their four month old has tasted spinach yet. It is just not that important.

More and more parents are gaining confidence in their own ability to make decisions about their children; they are learning to trust their own instincts in matters of childbirth and child raising. They are learning not to be constantly swayed by the opinions of "experts."

This book contains the latest updated information on the baby food industry and why you should take an active interest in your baby's diet. We have included new information on breastfeeding. There are suggestions to help you prepare pure baby foods conveniently and at reasonable prices. The recipes have been selected with the entire family in mind and are popular with several age groups. Included are some old family favorites plus brand new ones thought up by friends and relatives—even one created by our ten year old son and his friends to relieve the tedium and heat of Washington, D.C. summers. And, because the future child is so sharply influenced by the mother's health, there are also some thoughts on a prenatal diet to assure the mother's health and the best physical and mental start in life for baby.

We hope you not only find something in this book to spur you down the road to good nutrition but all the information you need as to why you should go down that road, should anyone question your right to do so.

Mary Dustan and James S. Turner
Washington, D.C.
December, 1976

PART I

GETTING IN GEAR

A GENERAL OVERVIEW

This book was originally written as a partial answer to the hundreds of questions about food directed to us since publication of Jim's book, *The Chemical Feast*, the Nader Report on the Food and Drug Administration (FDA). That book outlines in some detail the failure of the FDA to maintain the quality and safety of the American food supply at the level which most people assume it should be maintained.

The main thesis of *The Chemical Feast* has been underlined by a number of discouraging incidents: mercury and Kepone have turned up in fish; botulism in pizza and cans of soup, and salmonella in well-known candy bars. Red dyes, numbers two and four, and carbon black, coloring used in thousands of foods for dozens of years, have turned out not to be safe enough to allow in food.

DES (diethystilbesterol), has been used in millions of cattle as a growth enhancer, and given to women in pill form during pregnancy to prevent miscarriages. Recently doctors have discovered that females born of these women are developing vaginal cancer during their teen years. Treatment for this cancer often involves a complete hysterectomy. There is even newer evidence which suggests precancerous conditions developing in the male children as well. Government regulators have not yet been able to ban its use.

Now that more people have become aware of the quality and safety problems which can be carried in their food supply delivery system, they are asking how the problems can be avoided. To begin with, one should avoid paranoid obsessions. Death and disability do not ride on every forkful of food. At the same time one should maintain a healthy skepticism of food industry assertions that all is perfectly well in the nation's canneries. These assertions fall continuously like a soft spring rain from the food pages of the nation's press and from dozens of magazines that derive a substantial part of their income directly from the food industry advertisements.

On the other hand, merely because someone has been called a faddist does not make him or her one. It has long been the practice of many in the food establishment to assume that those who criticize the American food supply must be somehow peculiar. Nor is this a totally unreasonable assumption, since the American food supply performs remarkably well in getting large amounts of different kinds of food to more people than ever before in history. However, treating food supply critics as peculiar overlooks the most important of American traits. Americans constantly insist that yesterday's triumph be bettered. In the case of the American food supply, recent events suggest that their desire ought to be fulfilled rapidly. The very successes of the food industry have made easier the distribution of food poisoning, contamination and low-nutritional quality. Those who point out potential problems can no longer be dismissed without careful consideration of their views.

The issues involved in choosing a safe, wholesome and nutritious meal for a family are complicated and much more important to most individuals than the foreign policy maneuverings of the nation (the slightest ripple of which leads to hundreds of hours of writing and commentary, including overviews, backgrounds, assessments, objections, endorsements and anecdotes) to which Americans are routinely subjected.

DO WE HAVE ENOUGH FOOD

Some Americans assume their supply of food to be adequately abundant, if not unlimited. This is one assumption under heavy assault by facts. Until 1972 little evidence challenged the satisfaction America felt about its abundance of food. That year unexpected events converged into a vigorous assault.

The weather on every continent—drought in India, frost in the Soviet Union, excessive rain in the United States—cut into the world's food producing capability. The Peruvian fish catch, usually the largest in the world, suddenly dropped dangerously. This drop in turn led to the shortage of poultry and livestock feed, since fish-meal makes up this feed.

At the same time the Soviet Union bought an unprecedented 28 million tons of grain, mostly from the United States, thus reducing American food stores. By this time the famous United States food surpluses, that had been the world's insurance against hunger, had virtually disappeared. By 1974 the United Nations' Economic and Social Council concluded that it "is doubtful whether such a critical food situation has ever been so world-wide."[1]

Increased population world-wide causes much of the problem too and although the United States has finally begun to get its population growth down toward acceptable rates the rest of the world has not yet followed suit. However, we now contribute to the problem of food availability in a different way: our affluence. Americans do not have their nation's wealth under control. For example, meat consumption means inefficient use of grains—affluent countries feed one third of their grain to animals. This fact caused Dr. George Borgstom of Michigan State University to say that "the livestock of the rich world is in direct competition (for food) with the humans of the poor world."[2] The article is an extensive and useful review of the world food situation.

But the facts affect American parents even more critically. "Even in the affluent U.S.," points out Thomas Canby in this review of world hunger in *National Geographic,* "poverty spells undernourishment for an estimated ten to twenty million." That approaches being 10 percent of the population. "Hardest hit," he goes on, "are children, whose growing bodies demand 2½ times more protein, pound for pound, than those of adults."[3]

In examining the problem of world-wide hunger, the abandonment of breastfeeding by mothers looms larger and larger as a cause of malnutrition. Dr. Alan Berg, Senior Nutrition Advisor for Agricultural and Rural Development of the World Bank, says "Mothers milk is the best and safest of all foods. Buying enough formula or cow's milk to replace it could consume a quarter to a half of a laborer's wages in the needy nations. Aside from the cost in lives, foregoing available mother's milk represents an economic loss likely to be in the billions of dollars annually."[4]

The way Americans feed their baby's contributes directly to this problem. Since affluence, particularly American-style affluence, has led to the reliance of parents on formula and baby foods, these products have come to mean status to parents in developing nations. Dr. Berg says the reason for the decline of breastfeeding is "partly because the bottle has become a status symbol."[5]

Sticking to breastfeeding is the first step in providing food that is the safest, most convenient and nutritionally best product for your baby. By contributing to the trend against bottlefeeding you can contribute to the effort to get more and better food to the rest of the world.

While feeding your baby you are an intimate part of a large chain of people whose individual actions add up to more or less general well-being of all people. Remembering that might help you feel less isolated and helpless in the face of global problems like the hunger crisis.[6]

THREE
BASIC
PRINCIPLES

This book is based on three principles about feeding babies: infants have rights,* each infant is a unique individual, and all individuals must feel secure about the quality of food they eat—or feed their children.

One of the basic rights of an infant from which all others flow concerns its nourishment. The baby's needs should be the primary consideration of its parents when they decide what, when, where and how often to feed their child. This infant right, and its parents' responsibility, includes the recognition that feeding performs a larger function than merely providing nutrients.

Secondly, each infant is a unique individual. This uniqueness challenges the marketing assumption by baby food companies that they can produce a food fit for the "average" baby thereby making it proper for all babies.

*This concept has been most effectively developed in a book essential for all parents of infants called *The Rights of Infants* by Margaret Ribble, M.D., published by the Columbia University Press. It should be in every parent's library.

Thirdly, individuals, including infants, must have adequate safeguards to assure that the food they consume will produce the benefits claimed by the company, wihout causing negative side effects. Therefore, the burden of establishing the safety of the substances added to baby foods and the quality of the finished baby food products rests with the baby food processing industry.

ARE INFANTS' NEEDS BEING MET

Once you accept the three basic principles of this book you will most likely raise questions about the way infants' and children's needs are currently met by the American food system. In November, 1969, the *Journal of Nutrition Education* released the results of one of the most important nutrition studies ever concluded. It reviewed all studies of vitamin and mineral nutrition that had been conducted in the United States between 1950 and 1968. The study is of great importance, not only because of the long period of time it covers, but also because, quite by chance, it deals mainly with middle-class Americans.

The findings startled even the researchers who began their effort before poor nutrition was a topic of national debate. They found that:

> Although the amount of data on nutrient intakes of infants is inadequate for sweeping generalizations, available reports sug-

gest that appreciable percentages of infants are poorly nourished and infants from high socio-economic groups may receive less adequate diets than those from low socio-economic groups.[1]

The study showed that dietary habits of the American public have steadily become worse, especially since 1960. (The last survey of the dietary habits of American households taken in 1965 and published in 1968 revealed a significant increase in the consumption of soft drinks, candy and desserts, and a drop in the consumption of milk and fresh vegetables between 1955 and 1965. The Department of Agriculture, which attempts to run a survey of this kind every 10 years, will again question consumers about their food consumption in 1977.) For example, nearly all children under one year of age have an iron intake less than the recommended dietary allowance and many families are not feeding their infants adequately.

These findings formed only part of a growing body of evidence of bad American eating habits. In response to all the evidence, former President Richard M. Nixon convened the White House Conference on Food, Nutrition and Health in Washington, in December, 1969. Dr. Jean Mayer was appointed as director. (Dr. Mayer is, at present, President of Tufts University.)

The Conference panel concerned with pregnant and nursing women and young infants noted that:

Vital statistics of the United States indicate a major shortage of national resources for medical and nutritional support committed to the pregnant woman and the infant. Data on the numbers of pregnant women who lack adequate maternity care, the prevalence of preventable complications of pregnancy, the incidence of death in infancy indicate serious prejudice by our national posture to the health of pregnant women and the growth and development of infants and children.[2]

The Conference Forum on Parents and Children described how bad the situation had become:

We like to think of America as a child centered society, but our actions belie our words. A hard look at our institutions and way of life reveals that our national priorities lie elsewhere. The pursuit of affluence, the worship of material things, the willingness to accept technology as a substitute for human relationships, and the readiness to blame the victims of evil for the evil itself have brought us to the point where a broken television set provokes more indignation and more action than a broken child.

America's children and their families are in trouble, trouble so deep and pervasive as to threaten the future of our nation. The source of the trouble is nothing less than a national neglect of children and those primarily engaged in their care—

American parents—Children and Families come last.[3]

Nutritionally, infants and their families too often come last. Many of the indicators of child neglect cited by the White House Conference—infant mortality, mental retardation, birth defects and nutrient deficiencies—can be traced in part to poor dietary habits. These habits, in turn, stem from a too easy acceptance of technological assumptions designed for the well-being of the economy, rather than of the people themselves. Hopefully, new ways of thinking about how to feed infants will force their parents to reconsider some of the assumptions they now hold.

INFANT DIETARY PROBLEMS

Writing in *The Home Birth Book* in 1976, Dr. Russell J. Bunai, points out that "the United States leads all other developed countries in the rate of infant deaths due to birth injuries and respiratory distress (neonatal asphyxia and other causes). According to the National Association for Retarded Children, there are about six million retarded individuals in the United States, and a predicted annual increase of over 100,000 per year. There also appears to be a progressive rise in the number of children with perceptual and behavioral disorders."[4]

Dr. Bunai suggests that hospital birth management practices are largely responsible for the relatively poor showing of Americans in the area of infant and fetal health. However, he does identify malnutrition in pregnant women as one of the primary contributions to developmental abnormalities of the fetus. Other doctors suggest that diet contributes measurably to perceptual and behavioral disorders.

In particular, Dr. Ben F. Feingold believes that hyperactivity in children, which seems to be on the increase, comes from and can be controlled by dietary intake. Dr. Feingold found that a number of his hyperactive child-patients improved markedly when artificial colors and flavors were removed from their diets.

Dr. Feingold suggests problems for infants as well. He found that nearly all pediatric medicines contained artificial flavors and colors. More importantly, he found that a large number of his hyperactive child-patients had begun life consuming infant vitamins. "They began with spoon-fed liquid drops, usually artificially colored and flavored, then shifted to the chewable variety at the age of a year or so. Several brands of drops show up like clockwork during infancy of a number of hyperactive children."[5]

THE PRENATAL DIET

The relationship between newborn child and mother, according to Dr. Margaret Ribble, is "a personal relationship on which the child's future emotional and social reactions are based." Years of study at the Boston Psychopathic Hospital and with Anna Freud in Vienna led Dr. Ribble to conclude that "motherly love is as vital to the child's development as is food."[1]

Food and love—that seems simple enough. Both the emotional and physical future of an individual depend on satisfying early needs. The argument goes further, asserting that satisfaction of these needs, both emotional and physical, is achieved in direct relation to the way that a child is fed. Thus begins the development of sound mental and physical health.

Feeding begins earlier than most people suspect. It begins even before the majority of women know that they are pregnant. Most women realize they are pregnant between the fourth and sixth week after conception. They then begin the routine protection of their future infant. If conscientious, they cut out smoking, stop taking tranquilizers and other drugs and change dietary habits. But by six weeks much of importance to their child has already occurred. It is a most critical period.

Often it is during the first or second week of pregnancy that a woman, unaware that she is pregnant, decides that she must lose the extra pound or two she has gained, "before she gets pregnant." At the very time when her beginning infant needs increased nutritional supplies she cuts them down. During the first month the fertilized egg increases 40 times in weight and 3,000 times in size. In this time it develops a head, body, the beginnings of organs and the foundation of what will later become the nervous system.

Between 18 and 24 days, the nervous system and brain need vitamin B_6 and B_{12}, proteins and body sugar for proper development. In addition, by about the seventeenth day, vitamin E and iron are essential to insure proper working of the red blood cell system to carry critically needed oxygen throughout the new forming body. By the twenty-fourth day the heart begins to pulsate, requiring calcium to do its work. At this stage the cartilage system (eventually to become the skeleton) requires vitamin B_2 and B_6, pantothenic acid and folic acid. By the end of the seventh week developing eyes require sufficient amounts of vitamin A. Between the seventh and ninth weeks teeth begin to form, and the cartilage turns into bone. Both processes require adequate supplies of phosphorus, calcium and vitamin D.[2]

Improper nutrition during the first weeks after conception can lead to health problems for both the mother and the child. Lack of iron may result in anemia for both. Lack of calcium can affect the child's dental health for life. Lack of folic acid, also very common in pregnancy, can affect protein construction and the basic chemicals of heredity. It is literally *vital* that any woman likely to get pregnant should be sure her diet includes all the nutrients needed during the first stages of pregnancy. The nutritional environment is established even before conception.

Eating habits undergo natural changes with the onset of pregnancy. Women notice a mild loss of appetite and feel full after eating. They then often tend to cut down on eating. Actually the feeling of fullness must be reconciled with the growing nutritional demands of the developing embryo. Eating several, perhaps five or six, smaller meals a day can accomplish this. Physician Benjamin Spock and nutritional expert Dr. Miram E. Lowenberg have prepared a sound recommended diet to meet this need.[3] Although prepared by Doctors Spock and Lowenberg in 1955 and more than 20 years old it remains valid, probably because it was based on observations of many pregnant women.

DIET ADAPTED FROM SPOCK AND LOWENBERG

Each meal you eat should have a good protein food. Protein is the most essential nutrient for the developing individual. Include milk, meat, eggs, cheese, or fish at each meal.

There are some serious, but as yet unresolved, questions about the advisability of both adults and

children drinking large amounts of cow's milk
which has not been heated to a hot temperature first.
Therefore, where possible, substitute yogurt, cottage cheese, homemade custard or any of our recipes
which contain milk. When milk is used as a drink,
such as before going to bed, make sure that it is
heated.

The questions concerning milk include what
some pediatricians see as a higher incidence of allergies among heavy milk drinkers, and mucus conges-
tions of the upper nasal passages. Dr. Russell Bunai
has done extensive studies on the effects of milk.
Perhaps your doctor would like to consult with him
on this issue. His address is 11125 Rockville Pike,
Rockville, Maryland.

The first meal of the day on a prenatal diet can
be an early breakfast. If it includes one egg, oatmeal
cooked in milk and served with milk, or one cup of
hot milk with cocoa as a beverage, that first meal
will fulfill its nutritional responsibility to the pregnant woman and her coming child.

It is not unusual for pregnant women to be hungry two hours after such a breakfast. So about 10
o'clock in the morning the second meal can be
eaten. It should be a regular meal, eaten leisurely,
and can consist of another glass of milk or a juice, a
cheese sandwich, or a piece of fruit, or some raw
vegetable like celery.

Lunch at noon should include cheese, fish,
meat or eggs, and another glass of milk. A meat and
vegetable soup or a fruit and vegetable salad would
be useful at this meal. Fruit is an important replace-
ment for those sweet desserts you may be craving.

By about four o'clock it may well be time for meal number four. Again a cup of milk, perhaps mixed with tomato soup, or a glass of orange juice, plus some fruit or melba toast (thin). If you must have sweets, one tablespoon of honey on the toast should do the trick. You'll be surprised at how it satisfies your sweet tooth.

By six it's time for dinner. This meal should be built around a good serving of meat, a cooked vegetable and, if desired, a potato. Be sure to include a glass of milk if one was skipped at four o'clock. The dinner meal can be exchanged with lunch if eating the major meal at noon is easier or more desirable. Finally, a bedtime snack is a must. A glass of hot milk plus a piece of fruit will do.

Below is a summary of the Spock-Lowenberg diet. A whole day's nutritional requirements can be provided by:

- four cups of milk (increased to six when breastfeeding).
- one quarter pound of lean meat—beef, lamb, pork, veal, liver, fish or poultry
- two eggs
- three servings of fruit—a serving is one medium-sized orange, one-half grapefruit or two large tangerines, the juice of one medium-sized lemon or 4 ounces of orange or grapefruit juice. Fruit selection should be varied according to the season, and personal preference.
- one medium-sized potato
- one dark green or bright yellow vegetable and one raw vegetable
- three servings of bread or whole grain cereal

- no more than two tablespoons of butter
- no candy, cookies or soda
- a daily vitamin supplement if and as pre-scribed by your doctor

FURTHER SUGGESTIONS FOR A HEALTHY PRENATAL DIET

In addition to the basic prenatal diet listed here you might want to consider some of the new information current in the field of nutrition.

It is important to always eat a variety of foods in order to fulfill your body's needs. Therefore, try not to eat the same things every day. For example, if you have eggs for breakfast one morning, have buckwheat pancakes or one of the interesting new dry granola cereals the next. Here are our sugges-tions culled from the latest nutritional findings. We do not use canned or frozen items unless it is difficult or impossible to find the same items fresh.

Milk. Instead of four cups of milk drink other acceptable liquids plus milk as well. This can in-clude fresh fruit juices, weak teas, or even water. Consider taking a calcium tablet in order to get the calcium needed for your growing fetus, rather than drinking so much milk. Remember to discuss this with your doctor first.

Meat and Fish. Vary your selection each day. Include plenty of fresh fish. Make sure you eat fresh pork, not sausages with additives and sugar, not cured hams or bacon and certainly not hot dogs or bologna or other processed luncheon meats.

Grains and Eggs. Instead of eating two eggs each day you can get your protein from other sources such as nuts, seeds and whole grains. There is much discussion now about unrefined stone-ground whole grains. Make sure you eat the three servings Spock and Lowenberg suggest, but they can be as muffins, breads, pasta, crackers or plain as cereals. Cereal with fruit makes a hearty breakfast or a good snack. Vary the grains you use and choose from:

Millet—use as a cereal topped with a dash of sesame seeds

Rye—great baked in crackers

Barley—boiled in soups

Buckwheat—use in pancakes instead of whole-wheat

Whole-wheat—this includes raw bran and wheat germ added as a topping

Soy flour—heavy by itself, great in combination with another flour

Oats—a good hearty dish of hot oatmeal is still an excellent breakfast (use stone-ground oats, not the kind labeled "quick cooking")

Rice—unpolished brown rice is more nutritious than white

Salads and Vegetables. They should become part of your daily diet and later you will want to accustom your children to eating at least one salad of fresh raw greens and vegetables each day. A large salad can make a delicious lunch all by itself. Always use the freshest ingredients you can find. Look for foods in season; they are delicious and usually cost less at that time. Remember to wash and dry each item carefully. Vary your lettuce selection to include chicory, escarole, endive, Boston, Bibb, iceberg and others. Season with fresh lemon juice, oil, pepper and herbs. Avoid using salt.

To your basic lettuce salad add any of the following or a combination of a few:

Sliced tomatoes in season

Fresh chopped mushrooms

Grated carrots, beets, parsnips, turnips

Dry-roasted unsalted soy beans or boiled garbanzo beans (chick-peas)

Sunflower and pepita (pumpkin) seeds

Sliced green pepper, eggplant or avocado

Radishes and celery

Parsley, bean sprouts, watercress

Cauliflower or broccoli heads

Young raw fresh dandelion greens or spinach

Fruits. Vary your intake of fresh fruit so that in any given week you have sampled as many as the season has to offer. Do not forget to sample fruits you may be unfamiliar with including papayas, persimmons, mangoes or figs. We do feel it necessary to warn against eating grapes. They are very heavily sprayed and we suggest you cross them off your list.

PRENATAL MEAL WITHOUT MEAT OR MEAT PRODUCTS

Here is a sample high-protein main dish which does not include meat, milk, eggs or cheese.

1 *tablespoon safflower oil*

1   *cup brown rice*
1   *tablespoon sesame seeds*
1   *tablespoon sunflower seeds*
¼   *cup almonds, chopped slightly*
1   *tablespoon raisins*
    Dash of nutmeg and cinnamon to
    season

Heat the oil in a saucepan. Combine all the other ingredients except for the raisins and sauté in the hot oil for a minute or two. Stir the ingredients so that they do not stick and each gets a slight coating of oil. This will help to seal in the flavor and the nutrients. Add 3¼ cups of water and bring to a boil. Lower the heat, cover the saucepan and cook until the rice is soft and the water gone. This will take approximately 45 minutes. Do not stir rice while cooking. Stir in the raisins and season with a little nutmeg and cinnamon.

If you prefer your raisins "plumped" add them to the rice combination when you add the water.

This dish also tastes good with raw pecans, cashews, peanuts or walnuts. Vary to taste.

FOR THE WORKING MOTHER-TO-BE

Even if you are working, you can manage to eat six meals a day. Breakfast, dinner and a late night snack can be eaten at home. Lunch plus a midmorning and midafternoon snack can be prepared at home and carried with you to the office.

It is better to eat a little every three hours than to eat a large lunch which sits in your stomach all day. Choose simple broiled meat or fish dishes rather than those which include heavy sauces. Sandwiches on fresh whole-wheat bread with bean sprouts instead of lettuce, or homemade chunky soups make lovely lunches.

Below are some easy snack suggestions for you to prepare:

Fresh vegetable sticks—carrots, celery, cucumber, zucchini squash, green pepper.

Tomatoes in season

Hardboiled egg

Fresh fruits such as apples, peaches, oranges or pears.

Sunflower seeds, raisins and nuts mixed together

Use your imagination to dream up concoctions to carry in a wide-mouthed thermos jar. Melon balls rolled in shredded coconut (not the kind with added sugar) are a good example of a refreshing and satisfying snack.

CUSTOM-MADE FOR MOTHERS

In 1970, Agnes Higgins of the National Montreal Diet Dispensary in Montreal, Canada, reported her observations of pregnant women and their children, conducted as part of a pilot nutrition and pregnancy program. Her general recommendations for a diet nearly matched those of Spock and Lowenberg. However, Higgins pointed out firmly—and every individual including prospective mothers should remember this—that general dietary recommendations can be misleading. Dietary needs are individual needs. One person's deficiency may possibly turn out to be another's excess.

The Montreal Diet Dispensary does individual dietary profiles to find what diet problems each individual pregnant woman has. Diets are then prescribed to meet these needs. This program is designed to prevent disease.

In Canada it is estimated that it costs $100,000 (per average lifespan) for the state to care for disabled, sickly, retarded or otherwise-ill individuals. On the other hand, it costs only $125 to properly analyze and provide for the additional nutritional needs a woman has during her nine month pregnancy. These supplements to the woman's diet, plus a rebudgeting of her money to provide foods for correct nutritional balance, can eliminate much costly sickness and disability.

First a trained nutritionist at the dispensary takes the patient's age, height and bone structure (small or large) and using a standard table computes her ideal weight. With this weight the nutritionist then computes calorie, protein and vitamin needs for the individual mother. Working with this information, plus awarding the pregnant woman the $125 diet supplement, dispensary workers have recorded standard weight gains of between 20 and 25 pounds, as was recommended by the National Research Council of the National Academy of Science.

After giving birth the mothers on the average have gained between four to nine pounds above their pre-pregnancy weight. The nine pound gains were by women who started the program slightly underweight; the normal weight gain was about four pounds. It has been the experience of the nutritionists at the Dispensary that this weight gain is what nature supplies to make breastfeeding possible. Those mothers who breastfed lost the four pounds within a few weeks.

The basic idea of the Montreal program makes great sense. If the diets of farm animals are prepared with scientific care as a part of the effort to produce prize-winning blue-ribbon cattle of outstanding size, strength and agility, why can't scientific feeding of humans produce healthier babies? From this simple premise grew the notion that nutrition is the most important factor, aside from genetics, in pregnancy and labor, accounting for growth, development and death rate. The experience of the Montreal clinic since 1962 shows that good nutrition can overcome serious problems of poverty and poor health backgrounds. Larger and healthier babies—averaging seven and a half pounds—were consistently produced by mothers eating nutritionally superior diets.

Mrs. Higgins also argues that toxemia, a disease of the latter half of pregnancy, is nutritionally related. She has observed women in her clinic with symptoms of toxemia—a weight gain during the last half of pregnancy of up to five pounds a week (the normal should be about one pound). Their diet histories showed low calorie and low protein intake.

When this was changed to a nutritionally balanced diet, high in protein and calories, weight gain came down to normal.

A California physician, Dr. Thomas Brewer, has written extensively in support of this idea. Eating nutritionally balanced foods is far more important than attempting to keep weight down artificially by the use of drugs or nutritionally poor diets.

PART II

WHAT YOU SHOULD KNOW ABOUT THE BABY FOOD INDUSTRY

NUTRITIONAL IGNORANCE

The food supply in the United States has become an unrecognized national crisis. Dr. Roger Williams, a noted expert on the chemical basis of nutrition and discoverer of pantothenic acid, a vitamin, has stated in his book *Nutrition Against Disease,* that:

> The food industries, though based on science, have tended to stand still (or regress) with respect to performing their essential function in society, namely, producing food of better nutritional quality for the consumers. Because of long-standing neglect of nutrition and the nutritional improvement of life, the food industries tend to take food quality for granted.
>
> There is a sore need for a revolutionary change in attitude. The public, the medical profession, those who produce food by agriculture, and those who process, package, preserve, distribute and sell foods, all need to realize that the quality of the food we eat is a problem that outranks even that of the quality of what we read in school books, newspapers and magazines.[1]

Leaders of the nutrition profession besides Dr. Williams have often decried the low level of nutrition education. Dr. Jean Mayer, President of Tufts University, has called America "a nation of nutritional illiterates." Dr. Fred Stare of Harvard School of Nutrition, Dr. W. Henry Sebrell, Director of the Institute of Nutrition Science of Columbia University, and Dr. Grace Goldsmith, former Chairman of the Food Nutrition Board, have all publicly lamented the fact that doctors have so little nutritional education. What has not been clearly recognized until recently is how pervasive the negative results of this ignorance have become.

It was not until the results of a survey of household food consumption by the Department of Agriculture, conducted in 1965, that evidence of widespread nutritional deficiencies began to receive public notice. Studies conducted by the Department of Health, Education and Welfare under the direction of Dr. Arnold Schaffer discovered large geographical pockets of undernourished individuals—the complete results of these studies have yet to be released. News media began to give wide coverage to the growing awareness of the problem of hunger in America, and the White House Conference on Food, Nutrition and Health was convened in December, 1969.

Looking back on the events of 1969 four years later, in 1973, Dr. Ross Hume-Hall, former Chairman of the Biochemistry Department at McMaster University in Ontario, Canada, saw little progress. In his book, *Food For Nought,* he states, "The White House Conference . . . singled out for attention pregnant and nursing women and young children . . . however the report and its recommendations remain sequestered in the bowels of government bureaucracy." Dr. Hume-Hall explains why: "The objective of the food industry is to develop palatable products that sell well; nutritional factors, in their opinion, contribute nothing to palatability, so they are ignored."[2]

We cannot continue to ignore these factors vital to the health of our babies, and thus to the health of our nation.

Now there is a general awareness that all is not as it should be in the development and distribution of the nation's food. But the real implications of the problem have not yet been fully appreciated. In Dr. Williams' paper to the National Academy of Science in 1970, "Should the Science-based Food Industry Be Expected to Advance?," he made the point that general information well-known to nutritionists had not yet been translated into practical usefulness by the food industry.

The baby food industry is a good example of his general observation. In both the kind of food it makes—relying on the use of several questionable food additives—and in the way it distributes food, the baby food industry demonstrates its lack of up-to-date scientific knowledge. The World Health Organization made explicit observations about the use of additives in baby food in 1962:

> Foods that are specifically prepared for babies require separate consideration from all other foods as regards the use of food

additives and toxicological risks. The reason for this is that the detoxicating mechanisms that are effective in the more mature individual may be ineffective in the baby. The Committee strongly urges that baby foods should be prepared without food additives, if possible. If the use of a food additive is necessary in a baby food, great caution should be exercised both in the choice of additive and in the level of use.[3]

In spite of such explicit observations the baby food industry still attempts to justify the continued use of various food additives. This is discussed in detail in the chapter entitled, "You Don't Always Get What You Need."

An even more basic conflict exists between the nutritional and economic purposes of the baby food industry. Nutritionally, baby food should provide food value for babies. Economically, baby food provides profits for industry and the producers of the baby foods have decided that to keep profits up they must expand their market beyond babies. Therefore, the industry tries to push convenience to parents and texture to the elderly. It tries, with its advertising to expand the baby feeding cycle to include the newborn infant and the young child beyond the baby food stage.

Dan Gerber, head of Gerber Foods, told *Forbes* magazine that "we think we can stretch the age group for our products to four or five years from the present infants."[4] The Beech-Nut Baby Food people developed fruit gels intended to "not only stimulate the use of baby food for children past the conventional baby-food stage, but . . . to have appeal to the adult's palate too."[5]

Seven to eight percent of Gerber's sales are to the elderly.[6] These foods are sometimes even prescribed for geriatric patients.[7] The Gerber's annual report in 1968 actually cited its research efforts to develop adult uses for baby foods. Spurred by what Gerber demographer William H. Francis calls the "birth dearth" (the declining American birth rate), this move to the adult market has taken on urgency.

Noting that adults or children—not infants—already consume 10 percent of all baby food, Gerber launched a major "Rediscover Gerber" advertising campaign in 1974, urging its fruits and desserts for coffee breaks, snack breaks, waffle toppings and the "sixty-second parfait." The advertisement ended with "Next time you are looking for a little something to eat, baby yourself with the unexpected snack." *Business Week* reported that in 1972 "Gerber shortened its slogan from 'Babies are our business . . . our only business' to 'Babies are our business'." In 1974, the slogan "disappeared completely from Gerber advertising."[8]

At the infancy end of the age spectrum, advertisements for baby food have been pushing the feeding of solids down to even earlier than one month. Dr. G.J. Fruthaler called this trend, "a fad based more on competitive instincts than scientific fact."[9] Helen A. Guthrie, writing in *Pediatrics,* reported that "A study by the Academy of Pediatrics revealed that physicians were advising the use of solid foods at earlier ages as much in response to the demands of mothers as on the basis of evidence that they were necessary for adequate nutrition. Processors of special infant foods may well have stimulated the demand for such a feeding program."[10]

It is also due to selling clever new products that have no more nutritional value than the products they replace. "We know," says Fred Yearky, vice-president of marketing at Gerber, "that your mother likes variety and she is susceptible to new products."[11] Selling to parents' susceptibilities does not place infant nutrition first on the priority list of infant food needs. In purely economic terms, expanding the baby food market has made nutrition more expensive for baby food consumers!

A THREATENED INDUSTRY

Early in 1976 the Baker/Beech-Nut Corporation president, Frank C. Nicholas, sent letters to 760,000 American mothers stating that spinach, carrots and possibly beets contained nitrates which could cause a condition in which "baby's skin turns blue and asphyxiation could result."

He also said homemade baby food lacked the nutrition of his products, citing documentation from "The University of California among others. . . ." He stated flatly that "Most homemade baby foods are not sterile." He claimed to make these statements because "Beech-Nut, as a responsible corporate citizen, feels compelled to speak out in the interest of safety and good nutrition for your baby." He supplied no scientific/medical evidence for his claims. In fact, there is no evidence to support his claims.

The Consumer Affairs Unit of the City of Syracuse, New York brought legal action in an effort to force the company to write retraction and correction letters to the mothers who received the company's letter. Unfortunately, a New York judge found that since Beech-Nut did not have offices in Syracuse,

Baker/Beech-Nut Corporation
2 CHURCH STREET • CANAJOHARIE, N.Y. 13317

FRANK C. NICHOLAS
PRESIDENT

Dear Mother:

Much publicity has appeared recently which urges mothers to make their own baby food at home. Some of this publicity is distributed by manufacturers of food grinders, blenders and other implements to sell grinders and blenders. Some is well-intentioned. Much is misinformed.

We at Beech-Nut feel obliged to advise you that some potential dangers for your child exist in the home preparation of baby food. Much of the publicity has been self-serving and has ignored this fact. Beech-Nut would never want to sell its product at the expense of the health and well-being of babies. That is why Beech-Nut, as a responsible corporate citizen, feels compelled to speak out in the interest of safety and good nutrition for your baby.

You, as a mother, should know that some cases of methemoglobinemia have been reported in medical literature from the feeding of home-prepared spinach puree, carrot soup and carrot juice. Beets may also be a problem.

Nitrates in these products can be converted to nitrites during transportation, from bacterial contamination or in baby's stomach which contains less acid than an adult's stomach. Nitrites combine with red blood cell pigments in a manner which prevents these pigments from performing their job of transporting oxygen to the body. With too much methemoglobin, baby's skin turns blue and asphyxiation could result.

Commercial blanching and processing eliminates most of the nitrates, eliminates bacteria and inactivates enzymes to prevent any remaining nitrates from converting to nitrites, thus eliminating the risk.

You, as a mother, should know that babies are more sensitive to bacteria than adults, and there is significant risk of bacterial contamination and resultant food poisoning in home-made baby food. Most

-over-

home-made baby foods are not sterile. Beech-Nut Baby Food is sterilized by heat and pressure cooking in hermetically sealed containers.

You, as a mother, should know that commercial baby food is adequate to the nutrition requirements of your baby. In contrast, do-it-yourself baby food loses nutrients four ways:

1. Through nutrient oxidation as a result of too much air inclusion, particularly when blenders are used.
2. Through pour-off of water-soluble nutrients.
3. Through use of raw foods of uncertain freshness.
4. Through freezing and thawing if food is made for subsequent meals.

The University of California, among others, has documented the greater loss of nutrients in home-prepared baby food compared to commercial products.

As a mother, you should know that Beech-Nut has dedicated over 40 years to making the purest, most nutritious baby foods using the best methods known to modern science and with the best medical advice available. Our standards in every case meet or exceed those established by federal and state regulatory agencies. Beech-Nut Baby Food contains no preservatives, artificial colors, artificial flavors or MSG. We assure you we will continue to make the best possible food for babies. We care.

Sincerely,

Frank C. Nicholas

Frank C. Nicholas
President

P.S. If you would like to know more or have any questions, please send me a note with your questions, or send your phone number and I or our technical people will be happy to call you at whatever time you indicate is convenient.

the City could not force the retractions. The case is on appeal. Three national consumer groups asked the Federal Trade Commission to order the corrective letters. The Commission has reached no decision yet.

In response to the furor over the original letter, Beech-Nut sought to clarify itself, saying it only wanted to warn about homemade spinach purée, carrot soup, carrot juice and beets. It cited Jean Mayer, at the time a nutritionist at Harvard University (and now President of Tufts University) to support its claims. Mayer in his syndicated newspaper column had written an article calling attention to a condition know as methemoglobinemia, which does cause blue skin and difficult breathing, but had not related it to homemade baby food.

Beech-Nut President Nicholas referred to the article and said "Home preparation obviously increases the risk in the U.S."[1]

Mayer became so concerned about the distortion of his writings that he wrote directly to the Syracuse Consumer Affairs Unit to "deplore the fact that an article of mine has been misused by a commercial baby food company." Mayer then wrote a special article saying that "nothing could be farther from the truth . . . (than Beech-Nut). . . . implying that I am not in favor of home prepared baby foods." He wrote that whenever asked by mothers "Is it all right to make my own baby food?". . . . I always answer with a resounding 'Yes'."[2]

Mayer indicated several simple precautions to follow. The suggestions in this book contain his precautions. In summary they are: use only fresh, wholesome food; observe the utmost cleanliness; wash and peel food carefully; do not salt or season foods for babies; feed carrots, beets and spinach only occasionally (and we would add, only after four months of age); store by freezing; and if you must use manufactured baby foods read the labels to avoid the outright junk.

The reaction to the Beech-Nut letter did not end with the Mayer column.

Contacted about the alleged evidence that manufactured baby food contains more nutrients than homemade baby food, the University of California had trouble locating any documentation to validate this premise. After writing to Mr. Nicholas, Helene Swenerton, University Extension Nutritionist, obtained a copy of what Beech-Nut based its assertion on. It turned out to be a study comparing commercially canned and experimentally frozen fruit and vegetable purées which appeared in *Food Technology* for March, 1949.

The study did not deal with homemade baby food. It was initiated in 1940, making it thirty-six years old when cryptically cited by Mr. Nicholas.

Dr. Samuel J. Fomon of the University of Iowa, commenting on the Beech-Nut letter, said "I was somewhat amused that Mr. Nicholas seems to believe that his Company can pour off the water containing the nitrates and the nitrites without pouring off water-soluble vitamins." He went on to say that unlike other companies, Beech-Nut had not supplied him and his colleagues with nutritional studies of its food. "I find it hard," he wrote, "to take seriously any statement suggesting that the

Beech-Nut Company is primarily interested in the welfare of infants.''[3]

Dr. Mayer deplored the use of his column to support Beech-Nut's nitrate scare tactics against homemade baby food; the reference to the University of California turned out to be specious; and Dr. Fomon threw cold water on the assertion that Beech-Nut Foods were known to be more nutritious than homemade foods. This left only the impression that the medical profession blessed processed baby food. The letter implied that the medical profession preferred manufactured to homemade baby food. The American Academy of Pediatrics soon put that Beech-Nut-created impression to rest.

The Academy Committee on Nutrition answered the letter on the Beech-Nut claims in February, 1976, in the Academy newsletter *News and Comments*. It said, "The Committee deplores scare tactics used either by industry or any other group and indeed is concerned in this case that some material from scientific publications has been taken out of context." The Committee went on to say, "The material on methemoglobinemia refers to very young infants, hardly old enough to be offered solid foods. Nitrates are present in conventional food stuffs. However, the amount of nitrates in conventional foods is unlikely to cause harm when fed to infants over four months of age unless the food is prepared in the presence of gross contamination."[4]

Concerning vitamin C content, the Committee pointed out that the higher amounts in some manufactured food results "Only because vitamins are added to the commercial product to replace vitamins lost during processing.'' The Committee also stated ''we are not in agreement with implied excessive dangers in home preparation of foods.''[5] In short, the American Academy of Pediatrics added its voice to the many others raised against both the general impression and the explicit statements of the Beech-Nut letter asserting the low quality and possible hazards of homemade baby food.

Unfortunately, the Beech-Nut letter, while more extreme than claims of other baby food companies, still represents a general industry strategy to attack the ability of parents to feed their families and to discourage them from making their own baby food.

GERBER TACTICS

Gerber mutes the arguments against parents but uses the same general themes in other ways. On the back of its baby cereal boxes, Gerber touts its ''high standards of bacteriological safety.'' It goes on to say ''home preparation involves significant risk of bacterial contamination.'' In its own magazine, *Pediatric Basics,* printed for use in doctors' offices, the company repeats the theme. In advertisements alleging that it takes 21 steps to prepare baby food at home and only three (the third is ''trust Gerber'') to use manufactured food, the Company speaks of ''undesirable enzymes'' and ''undesirable or dangerous bacteria'' which must be cooked out of foods at home—without destroying heat sensitive nutrients.

Gerber, like Beech-Nut, argues that homemade

baby food contains fewer nutrients than manufactured baby food and poses greater safety hazards. To these themes it adds the claim, on the back of its cereal box, that "Gerber has always sought and followed the guidance of doctors who are in active practice, research and teaching." This implies, though it does not directly claim, that the medical profession shares the Gerber view of its product as superior to the homemade variety. The facts do not support any of these three themes.

When Consumers Union checked the comparative nutrient value of processed versus homemade baby food in its laboratory, the homemade brand came out consistently ahead. Commenting on Gerber claims of homemade hazard, the Consumers Union wrote in *Consumers Reports,* "But the enzymes and bacteria found in fresh, clean foods are not harmful to an infant. And the baby food manufacturers themselves, in heating baby foods to the extreme temperatures used commercially to destroy enzymes and bacteria (which might cause an 'off' taste in the processed food), destroy many vitamins and minerals."[6]

Like Beech-Nut, Gerber makes unsupported claims about the safety and quality of its products as compared to homemade baby food. But it goes further when attempting to argue that making your own baby food is seven times more inconvenient than trusting Gerber. The argument is false. Four of the 21 steps in preparing homemade food include, according to the Gerber ad, "store carefully."

Interestingly, the back of the Gerber cereal boxes recommends almost exactly the same steps for storing Gerber products. Four other steps say "pick variety." The back of the cereal box says, "selections from the wide variety of baby foods help assure optimal nutrition." Whether fresh or Gerber foods are used, choices must be made to insure variety.

Two steps are to add just enough salt and sugar. But no sugar or salt should be added to homemade baby food. Four of the steps advise keeping the utensils and the kitchen clean. Consumers Union points out that these are done routinely on a daily basis anyway through scrubbing the kitchen and washing the dishes. (Is Gerber hinting that current American homemakers and parents are not clean enough?) Two steps are to use just enough but not too much water to boil and mix the foods. The boiling can be done with the family meal, and the mixing need not make water the most or second most prevalent ingredient. You do not need to use as much water as is used in most processed baby food. The two remaining steps are to avoid salted meats and contaminated leftovers. Neither seems insurmountable nor are they an inconvenience which warrants paying two and a half times more for the food you buy for your baby. In short, not only is the quality of their products debatable but Gerber's claims to convenience may also be questionable. And it doesn't stop there.

POOR PACKAGING

Late in 1971 Mrs. Richard Falk of Princeton, New Jersey, found worms in her baby food jars. She wrote to complain to Gerber and received a lot of baby food delivered to her house and a letter of apology. This response instead of placating, outraged her. She bought many jars of baby food and checked them for worms. She found worms in a number of them.

Again she wrote to Gerber. This time Gerber sent a Company representative to talk to Mrs. Falk. He said that retail stores and not Gerber caused the worms to be in the food. He carefully took the cigar from his mouth and sprinkled ashes around the edge of the Gerber jar. He then popped the lid, breaking the vacuum suction, causing the cigar ashes to be sucked into the baby food jar. This, he said, showed that lack of cleanliness in transportation, storage and display caused the problem and not the manufacturing by Gerber.

In its 1975 test of baby food, Consumers Union specifically warned about this deficiency. "In some instances," wrote CU, "Insect filth may have wound up in the tested foods because of a design deficiency. On certain baby food jars, there is a visible gap between the sides of the lid and the glass. Foreign matter tends to collect in this breach and is sucked into the jar when the vacuum seal is broken."[7] Thus CU and Gerber apparently agree on the problem. They only argue about the blame. At the very least an additional step, washing all baby food jars, should be added to steps in preparing processed baby food.

Consumers' Research Magazine, put out by a consumer testing group comparable to Consumers Union, reported in 1975 that the lid problem of baby food jars remained unresolved. While the Department of Agriculture requires (since December, 1975) meat products to be packaged in safe jars, no such regulation governs other baby food products. Since it can take years for a jar of baby food to be removed from the shelf of a supermarket, every baby food customer should examine jar lids carefully before buying.

Two additional sources of contamination by foreign matter exist. First, there appears to be a practice of loosening baby food jar caps by a minority of customers in retail food stores. Every jar should be checked to be sure that the lids are firmly in place. If the vacuum packed jars have been tampered with the lid will bulge upward and the jars should be taken to the manager of the store. This adds one or two more steps to the use of processed baby food.

The second additional source of contamination appeared in the 1975 Consumers Union test. The consumer testing group examined 16 jars of each brand of each food analyzed. In ten of the foods the group found insects, insect parts, and rodent hairs. In six of the foods it found between five and 15 paint chips broken off from the undersides of the jar lids. In one food there were 350 paint chips or more than 20 chips per jar. Consumers Union drops its guard somewhat when it claims that "The insect and rodent filth we found is not considered a health hazard."[8] This may be true for that which comes from the factory and goes through the cooking process. It cannot be true for that insect filth which the test group suggested might have come from the lip of the jars.

Baby food companies proclaim the superior nutritional value of their food. Testing evidence refutes the claim. Baby food companies either scare or confuse parents by saying homemade baby foods are less safe than processed varieties. Nutritionists and doctors rebut the claim with words such as "deplorable" and "unfortunate scare tactics." Baby food companies claim that their products are a picture of purity when in fact they can contain, and often do, insect parts, worms, paint chips and other foreign matter. The companies say it is harder to make your own baby food than use the processed kind, when this is not the case. Each of these misstatements in itself reveals an important failure in the baby foods' processing procedures. But taken together they reveal a serious and disturbing lack of regard for the ultimate consumer of baby food products. Baby food company claims cannot be taken at face value. Aside from the more serious potential health problems reported in the next chapter the attitude of baby food companies revealed by the arguments they make for their products should put every parent on notice.

King Features' columnist, Phyllis Battelle, writing of the Beech-Nut "scare prose" letter (as she called it) made clear the threat the companies see from parents who are skeptical about their product, and the silliness of their efforts to overcome the threat. "Rather than achieving the objective of nipping in the bud the slowly growing movement toward home-preparation of infant fare—[Beech-Nut] opened a can of worms in consumer and family circles. It is also turning out to be an enormous boost to the cook-it-yourself concept in baby feeding.

"The idea backfired. It is ironic that an inept and misleading flyer from a major U.S. corporation should backfire, giving great momentum to the trend they were trying—too desperately—to quench."[9]

Dr. Mayer reported in his column on the Beech-Nut letter that he is asked "more and more by young mothers these days"[10] whether it is all right to make your own baby food. As already reported, he has put his energy behind the homemade baby food method. Parents across the country are getting into the swing, learning that good nutritious meals can be made conveniently and inexpensively in their homes and while doing the preparation themselves they can protect their infants from hazards like salt, sugar, modified starch, and flavor enhancers like MSG/HVP, to say nothing of worms and rodent hairs.

YOU DON'T ALWAYS GET WHAT YOU NEED

Good reasons for avoiding processed baby food exist. Primarily, the companies manufacturing baby food have not been completely candid in their dealings with the public about fundamental issues of quality, safety and cost. It is difficult to know the proper answers to questions about the less than perfect performance of these products as food. But the baby food companies have seized upon this difficulty to create confusion and misunderstanding among the consuming public.

Critics of processed baby food raise the same basic policy questions that this book raises generally:

1. What is the best way to meet the individual needs of any baby—processed baby food?

2. In the absence of definitive knowledge about the safety and side effects of added chemicals, who takes the risk—babies?

3. What is the best way to properly handle a baby's reasons, both psychological and nutritional, for eating—processed baby food or its alternatives?

4. What is the best way to receive the highest

nutrition for the dollar—processed baby food or its alternatives?

Five separate controversies about additives over the past years illustrate the baby food companies' inadequate response to each of these basic questions. Each of five materials at one time added to baby food—MSG (monosodium glutamate), HVP (hydrolyzed vegetable protein), sugar, salt and modified starch—has been criticized. The baby food companies' responses to each of the criticisms suggested a greater concern on their part for profits than for quality or safety. But, before going briefly into the details of each of these controversies, they must be set against the background of two important facts.

First, in spite of their advertising and in spite of their efforts to stretch the use of baby food to older and older children, baby food manufacturers, when pressed, argue that they never intended their products to be more than a supplement to other methods of eating. Second, whatever the intention of the companies, baby food is an expensive substitute that, from the standpoint of cost, should be utilized only by those who have little concern over costs.

Dr. I. J. Hutchings, Director of Research for Heinz, comments:

> I don't think that the baby food industry has ever advocated that the mother cease breastfeeding and feed infant food. In fact, baby food is a supplemental food to breastfeeding—not in place of breastfeeding.[1]

Every parent should remember this statement when deciding how much and how often to feed a baby the products of Dr. Hutchings' company. He or she should also keep in mind some comparative cost figures for processed baby food.

THE COST FACTOR

In 1970, Ralph Nader reported the results of a shopping survey conducted by members of his Center for the Study of Responsive Law. They showed processed baby food to be much more expensive than the equivalent homemade varieties.

We repeated the same buying study in June, 1976, with the same results. Heinz baby applesauce sold for 3.75 cents an ounce. National brands of large bottles of adult applesauce ranged in price from 1.82 cents to 2.37 cents an ounce. Smart comparative buying can save between 1.93 to 1.38 cents an ounce, or up to 26.88 cents per 16 ounce jar. Fresh apples cost 39 cents a pound, or more than one third *less* than the baby applesauce with water added.

In 1976 three cooked egg yolks in a baby food jar, with water and iodized salt added, cost 39 cents. Three *whole* medium-sized fresh eggs cost 23.6 cents. Three AA large eggs cost 28.3. Egg yolks in baby food jars with water and salt added cost between 25 and 33 percent more than whole fresh eggs. Baby pears in jars with sugar added cost 63 cents a pound. Canned adult pears cost 39 cents a pound. Fresh pears cost 49 cents a pound. Baby pears cost 1.38 times the price of fresh pears and 1.65 times adult canned pears.

Canned baby squash, with water and salt cost 63 cents a pound, 2.17 times the price of fresh acorn squash. Baby food beef sold for $1.87 per pound. Fresh stewing beef sold for $1.35 per pound.

Gerber apple juice for babies cost $1.45 a quart. Regular apple juice could be bought for 45 cents a quart. Baby beef liver with liver broth cost $1.78 per pound. Fresh beef liver cost 79 cents per pound. Cottage cheese with pineapple for babies sold for $1.05 a pound and contained sugar, modified starch, nonfat dry milk, and pineapple, plus orange juice from concentrate, as well as its principal ingredients. Regular cottage cheese cost 59 cents a pound and canned pineapple cost 63 cents per pound. Baby oatmeal went for 63 cents a pound and adult oatmeal could be purchased for as little as 39 cents a pound. Orange juice from concentrate mixed up for babies went for $1.45 a quart. Adult orange juice concentrate from the frozen food counter (water to be added by you) cost 48.5 cents.

The specific figures are not the important part of this report. The principle that smart comparative buying saves money in the baby's feeding budget is important.

Make a shopping list of food for baby. Take note of the price of food on adult or regular packages, or the fresh produce forms and compare them to the price on baby food jars and boxes. Baby food costs nearly two and one quarter times more than the comparable regular food.

Dr. D. B. Jelliffe, when he was with the Caribbean Food and Nutrition Institute said, after some careful study of the initial report, "They (semi-solid infant weaning foods) can well form part of the diet of the well-to-do. For the less privileged, less affluent, they are a wasteful deviation of most limited resources. . . ."[2] At their best, baby foods, as spokesmen for their producers freely argue, act as a supplement—a rather expensive supplement—for other methods of feeding. Unfortunately, the failure of the baby food companies to effectively meet and refute arguments against the addition of five materials—MSG, HVP, salt, modified starch and sugar—to their products offers additional reasons for thinking twice about using processed baby food as the prime source for an infant's feeding.

MONOSODIUM GLUTAMATE

Monosodium glutamate (MSG) is a chemical used to enhance the flavor of foods. Until November, 1969, baby food companies added the substance, according to R. Burt Gookin, Chief Executive Officer, H. J. Heinz Company, to products because, "mothers were suspicious of food that didn't taste good. They didn't know whether it was meant to taste that way or whether there was something wrong with it. It soon became apparent that not only would the mother prefer those products that tasted good, but also that babies were influenced by the mother's attitude toward the food during feeding."[3] While MSG is no longer added to processed baby foods, the industry's attitude in handling suggestions (from informed sources) that it should be removed, provides us with an important insight into the baby food industry's behavior in general.

In 1969, Dr. John Olney, a psychiatrist at the Washington University School of Medicine, St. Louis, Missouri, stomach fed infant mice (under 20 days old) on MSG in amounts comparable to that in commercially prepared baby food. Dr. Olney tested MSG as one of a group of substances—known as neurological excitors—which act upon the central nervous system. The mice who ate the MSG developed brain lesions—as did other mice fed similar chemicals. Dr. Olney concluded that accumulation of this type of chemical in the cells of the developing central nervous system, "could trigger a neuro-degenerative syndrome (and subsequent mental retardation)."[4] He felt that such a possibility deserved further investigation, particularly since little is known about the causes of mental retardation. He urged that MSG be removed from baby food until his questions had been answered. The baby food industry responded with outrage to Dr. Olney's suggestion.

After a good deal of argument, the processors finally agreed to voluntarily remove the additive from their products. However, the MSG issue is still of importance to parents with infants. *No food containing MSG should be given to infants.* (In fact, any chemical with such physiological activity should be suspect for consumption by anyone.) When preparing homemade baby food, parents should not use MSG or foods containing MSG.

It should also be noted that although MSG was no longer added to processed baby foods, the jars containing it were not removed from supermarket shelves. Dr. Robert A. Stewart, Director of Research and Development at Gerber, explained, "We agreed not to manufacture baby food with MSG anymore, but we didn't agree to take what we had made off the shelves or out of the warehouses. We agreed to take out MSG, not because we think it is harmful—we don't—but because the public was upset."[5]

This attitude is typical of the baby food industry. It is one of the prime reasons why parents should be skeptical about company assurance that all their products are perfectly safe, highly nutritious and economic bargains. While no baby food companies would deliberately place unsafe chemicals in their products, their primary interest is in running a profitable business. As a result, small scientific indications that may ultimately prove to be of great significance to the babies eating their products aren't acted upon until "the public gets upset." The need to make a profit often conflicts with early scientific warning. That is why baby food companies must prove their products safe before they reach the market. Since the companies have not yet adopted this position, their products should be viewed with skepticism.

Concerning MSG, Dr. Olney was not the only scientist to raise questions about its safety. Dr. Jean Mayer, President of Tufts University, was nutrition advisor to President Richard M. Nixon during the

1969 White House Conference on Food Nutrition and Health. He has also seen the kinds of lesions reported by Dr. Olney in his own laboratory experiments. Two other scientists, T. W. Redding and A. V. Schally, reported injection studies in rats which produced "marked inhibition of endocrine function, including the increase in pituitary weight and its hormone content, atrophy of the sex, thyroid and adrenal glands with a retardation of growth and development of obesity."[6]

The National Academy of Sciences-National Research Council Committee reviewing the information on MSG has concluded that there is no evidence of any harm in feeding foods containing MSG to infants. According to the Gerber Company, "the chances of any such harm are extremely remote."[7]

Yet no one has explained satisfactorily why the chemical, along with others of a similar nature, has such a profound effect on the central nervous system of animals and even on adults as the increasingly well-known Chinese Restaurant Syndrome. Nor has anyone offered any clear hypothesis to explain the cause of most mental retardation. It is the hypothetical relation between these two uncharted facts that Dr. Olney is pursuing in his laboratories under a grant from the National Institute of Mental Health. Since MSG performs no nutritional function, it should be avoided in baby food. By leaving the MSG-containing baby foods produced prior to November 1969 on the grocery shelf, the baby food industry acted with less than prudence.

HYDROLYZED VEGETABLE PROTEIN

Sometime after the industry agreed (in 1970), in order to pacify the public, to remove MSG from baby food, a new ingredient, hydrolyzed vegetable protein (HVP) began to appear on baby food labels. Between then and December, 1975 Gerber made a total of 15 baby and toddler products containing HVP.

In fact, HVP contains free glutamic acid, the very substance which caused all the concern leading to the removal of MSG from baby food. Asked early in 1976 about the addition of HVP to Gerber products, Director of Research and Development, Dr. Robert A. Stewart, said it had not been added to foods since December, 1975. Asked why Gerber used HVP, he replied in a letter to a medical research journal "to enhance the flavor of foods."[8]

Gerber had found a way to get around public awareness and concern. When the public identified MSG as a substance to avoid, Gerber found a new substance, HVP, which provided the same flavor enhancing and raised the same questions, but which the public did not recognize as dangerous. Gerber went so far as to advertise, on the back of Gerber® Rice Cereal, that "Monosodium glutamate (MSG) is NOT added to Gerber Baby Foods." (Emphasis in the original.) Gerber made this claim while products containing HVP and its free glutamic acid occupied the shelf next to the rice cereal. *Companies that play loosely with public confidence deserve consumer skepticism.*

In the case of HVP Gerber removed the flavor enhancer without a public outcry. But the removal came only after an August, 1973 article by Dr. John Olney in the *New England Journal of Medicine* reporting on brain lesions in mice injected with hydrolysates used for intravenous feeding of hospital patients.[9] It came after the Food and Drug Administration (FDA) began an investigation into the safety studies on another amino acid product, aspartame, which in high doses had caused epileptic fits in monkeys. It came only after a December 4, 1975 correspondence to the *New England Journal of Medicine* from two medical researchers reporting on the apparent relationship between glutamate and the onset of epileptic fits and shivers in three children. (The researchers suggested that the condition of the three children [age six months, 16 months and 14 years] represented "some lesion in either the transport or the metabolism of glutamate that is challenged by concentrations of the flavor enhancer used both in packaged foods and the restaurant industry."[10])

One of the researchers wrote to the FDA and to Gerber about these findings. The Company answered that as of December 31, 1975 they discontinued the use of HVP in all new products (although they continued to market products already produced with HVP in them).

The suggestion that glutamic acid might have adverse effects on infants has been in medical literature for the better part of the past decade and continues to gain support. It seems inconceivable that Gerber would not know of this record, but ignored the warnings about HVP. As suggestions of adverse reactions related to free glutamic acid continued to accumulate, the use of HVP apparently became unacceptable to Gerber.

As long as food companies insist on avoiding prudence and candor in dealing with the public, the public should avoid its products whenever possible. If the baby food manufacturers acted with limited disregard for the public only on the MSG/HVP problem, that action could be deplored but acknowledged as the exception. Unfortunately, that insensitivity is not the exception.

SALT

The argument about salt is one of amount. Critics of baby food manufacturing practices argue that the amount of salt in processed baby food should not exceed the amount in breast milk. According to Dr. Jean Mayer, an infant raised on cow's milk consumes, on the average, three times more sodium than a breastfed infant. And, according to the National Academy of Sciences-National Research Council Report released in September, 1970, prepared baby meats and vegetables contained more than four times as much salt as cow's milk (250 milligrams per 100 grams compared to 58 milligrams per 100 grams). Prepared dry baby cereal contained nearly seven times as much salt as cow's milk (400 milligrams per 100 grams). This meant that some processed baby foods contained from twelve to twenty times as much salt as breast milk.

The Report recommended reduction of salt content in baby food. It suggested cutting salt content from 6.1 to 5.2 milligrams per 100 grams for mixed cereals with apples and bananas; from 3.1 to 1.0 for bananas; 36.0 to 18.9 for vegetables and beef; 52.5 to 44.0 for carrots; 35.8 to 1.9 for green beans; and 12.9 to 5.6 for chicken and vegetables.[11] The baby food industry indicated a willingness to go along with the recommendations although the manufacturers speak less than candidly about salt, much the same as they did with the MSG/HVP controversy. Salt is an essential nutrient and makes baby food more acceptable to infants, claims Gerber on the back of the 1976 Rice Cereal box. It also claims to now base its salting procedures on the 1970 National Academy of Sciences Report on salt in baby food.

These claims overstate the facts since the NAS Report made clear that companies added salt to baby foods "In order to increase acceptability of the food (to the mother)."[12]

Committee members justified their recommendation to substantially lower but not to eliminate salt by saying that it seemed "likely" to them that unsalted "foods would be salted to the mother's taste—resulting in variable and uncontrolled salt consumption." Thus it recommended the industry control the addition of "some salt to certain infant foods—particularly those that would most probably be salted by the adult."[13]

The entire argument supporting the NAS Report's recommendation rests on the assumption that parents are irresponsible and incapable of learning not to add salt to baby foods. There is no suggestion in the Report that any amount of salt added to baby food is essential for babies or that the addition of salt to baby foods makes it more acceptable *to babies*.

Consumers Union reported in the September, 1975, issue of *Consumers Report* that solid baby foods it tested contained on the average 132 milligrams of sodium per jar. A five month old infant required between 50 and 115 milligrams of sodium a day. Most of the products tested exceeded 150 milligrams per jar and several exceeded 200 milligrams per jar.

The 1974 edition of the *NAS Handbook on Recommended Dietary Allowances* (RDA) estimates that the average intake of a six month old American infant is approximately 805 milligrams per day. The *NAS Handbook* says that this amount is *"probably not greatly* in excess of the amount that would be provided from an equivalent caloric intake from whole cow's milk."[14] (The emphasis is ours.)

The Handbook authors try to reassure parents about salt by arguing that the amount consumed by their six month old infant is no higher than if their entire food intake were cow's milk. But this amount is seven to 16 times greater than the reported infant requirement and more than three times the amount which would be provided by a diet consisting totally of breast milk. If it were clear that excess salt posed no hazard, parents could be comfortable about these figures. It is not clear that excess salt poses no hazard.

In a special edition of January-February, 1976, *Mothers' Manual* a spokesman for Gerber said in defense of added salt, "One opinion holds that salt intake above the bare minimum requirement may lead to hypertension in later life. Animal experiments and epidemiological evidence can be cited to support this opinion."[15] He goes on to state that after reviewing the evidence the NAS committee recommended lower salt content of baby food and the industry complied.

This he claims ends the matter until further evidence changes it. As his Heinz Company counterpart stated in the same magazine story, "When changes in type and balance of food constituents are forthcoming from accepted authorities, we will certainly incorporate them in the baby foods."[16]

Such an argument makes a test case out of each baby food consumer. The 1974 NAS-RDA made clear that "moderate loads (of sodium) are promptly excreted . . . ."[17] in the average individual. However, it also makes clear that when these mechanisms break down, or when intake or losses exceed their abilities, disorders of sodium metabolism occur.

Relying on his argument for biochemical individuality, Dr. Roger Williams would challenge as relative such terms as "average" and "moderate." What is moderate or the average may be excessive for a number of individuals. The more one exceeds the necessary amount of sodium in the general diet, the more one takes the chance that an increasing number of individuals will move into the area of sodium metabolism disorders. The baby food industry seems to be asking its critics to prove excess sodium dangerous before it will take seriously the possibility that it is dangerous.

This reverses the logical order of the burden of proof. The NAS Committee, which is ambivalent on the matter of high salt inducing hypertension, flatly states in its 1974 edition of the RDA that "the blood pressure of hypertensive individuals is reduced on a diet low in salt."[18] A concerned parent might prudently reduce the salt intake of his or her infant rather than take the chance of becoming a statistic in the research that eventually leads to changes in baby food company policy.

But baby food companies make it hard to avoid excess salt. The 1974 RDA Handbook reports that "it should be noted that, since 1970, the amount of sodium chloride added to *many* infants' foods was decreased."[19] (The emphasis is ours.) Thus some baby foods apparently did not have their salt content decreased.

If the same procedure used on MSG is followed each time a baby food product has its salt content lowered, then each excessively salted product will remain on the shelf an average of two and perhaps as long as three or more years. Thus those products desalted on the day of the September, 1970, NAS Report might have remained on the shelf as long as

1973. Those products which might not have yet been desalted as of the publication of the NAS (1974) RDA-Handbook may remain on the shelves until at least 1977.

There is also an additional problem with salt. The 1970 NAS Committee specifically stated that "no increases should be made in salting those foods, such as fruits, that are now generally acceptable as currently prepared with less than 0.25 percent added salt."[20] Yet when Consumers Union examined commercial baby foods in 1975, six of 12 fruit and dessert products exceeded the amounts which the NAS had reported for such products in 1970.

The NAS Committee established the principle that only minimal amounts of salt necessary to prevent mothers from salting food themselves should be added to baby foods. The companies violate this principle in spirit in another way.

The range of salt among the same products made by different companies is staggering. Beech-Nut® Bananas with Tapioca contains nearly 15 times as much salt as the same product made by Heinz (seven as compared to 101 milligrams per jar). Conversely, Heinz® Chicken and Broth contains nearly two and one half times the salt of the same product by Beech-Nut (Heinz 175 to Beech-Nut 72 milligrams per jar). The same Gerber product contains 179 milligrams of salt. Gerber® Vanilla Custard Pudding contains two times the salt of the Heinz equivalent (Gerber 184 to Heinz 91 milligrams per jar). What's a parent to do?

The baby food companies make it impossible to

choose the low salt foods because they refuse to list the amount of salt contained in the product on the label. Until there are clear amount statements for such ingredients as salt, no one can be sure what amounts are included. Assurances by the baby food companies that they are complying with the best health requirements for infants must be treated with some doubt in view of their track record on other assurances to the public. The best approach may well be to avoid the habit of using baby foods which indicate on their labels that salt has been added to them. Of course, when you are preparing your own baby food, *do not add salt.*

MODIFIED STARCHES

Baby food producers also add modified starch, another troublesome material, to their products. Parents should avoid any food whose labels indicate that it contains modified starch. Baby food companies claim that they add modified starch to provide proper feeding texture and consistency. This task can be performed easily and effectively by using a kitchen blender. Critics of the baby food companies argue that modified starch is used solely for economic purposes. It extends the shelf life of baby foods, thus making them easier to market. The National Academy of Sciences-National Research Council (NAS-NRC) report on modified starches tended to support the critics on the purpose for modified starch:

Infant foods containing native starch undergo retrogradation; that is, the physical
bond between starch and water breaks
down, and water separates out of the col-
loidal suspension, resulting in a two-phase
liquid and semisolid system. Retrogradation shortens the shelf life of the product,
an important consideration under prevail-
ing marketing practices.[21]

Considerations important for the marketplace
are not considerations which come first on the priority list of infant needs. If parents buy food primarily
to meet their infants' needs, modified starches need
not be included in any of them.

If the use of modified starches raised no question about infant health or safety, it would be an
innocuous practice. However, it came under close
scrutiny after nutritionists pointed out to the
McGovern Committee (the Select Committee on
Nutrition and Human Needs, U.S. Senate) that the
increasing use of starch in baby food contributes to a
decrease in the amount of iron, copper and other
nutrients in the food. More importantly, critics of its
use pointed to certain experiments that suggested
that it was not well received by infant digestive sys-
tems. The critics urged that extensive studies be undertaken to determine how effectively infants digest
modified starch; researchers had found that infants
under six months do not digest at least one type of
modified starch efficiently.

The NAS-NRC report on modified starch did

not address this point. Rather it walked a narrow, and what many thought to be a misleading, scientific line. It found that, "There is no basis to conclude that the currently used modified food starches are less well metabolized than the native starches from which they are prepared; however, there is a lack of clinical evidence on this point."[22] If a parent ascribes to the principles that he or she does not wish to feed a child any substance until it has been established as safe, he or she should avoid any for which there is a lack of evidence. Modified starches fit the category of substances to be avoided in accordance with the principle that only those substances which are shown to be safe should be used.

One critic of modified starches summed up the situation in the memorandum to the McGovern Committee: "It may well be that additional studies will reveal that these modified starches are not as bad as they appear at this point. However, the thing that concerns us most is that they have found widespread use in infant diets and the proper questions regarding their metabolism by infants have not been asked."[23]

This memorandum was written in 1969, the NAS Report in 1970. Since that time baby food companies have undertaken no further studies of modified starches. Those points which lack clinical evidence in 1970 continue to lack clinical evidence. Those questions unanswered in 1970 remain unanswered. In fact, the baby food companies rest their defense of modified starch on the lack of evidence.

A spokesman from Beech-Nut summarized the industry position. "The modified food starches Beech-Nut uses are those which have been studied by the National Academy of Sciences and approved by the FDA," he told *Mothers' Manual* magazine in February, 1976. "Their purpose is to provide a consistency of texture which is important to acceptance of food by an infant and to ensure stability of product in storage,"[24] he added.

All three baby food companies, Gerber, Heinz and Beech-Nut say "the same modified starches have been used since 1970."[25] And they argue that no new guidance or regulations have been sought from the Food and Drug Administration. They are apparently satisfied that the questions unanswered in 1970 remain unanswered today.

In its 1975 study of baby food, Consumers Union raised three new points about modified starches. It pointed out that 25 percent of the solids in the food were modified starches, adding calories but not nutrients. It suggested that modified starches are especially suited to quick, high heat processing at baby food plants, adding a special economic advantage to baby food manufacturers. And it said that despite the specific warnings of the NAS "to test all new starches before use" the new modified starches in use today have never been fully tested for characteristics that might eventually affect babies.[26]

Baby food companies, of course, deny all these points. But once again the lack of candor and prudence which the industry reveals in its public comments and the unfounded attacks it launches against its critics suggest that their details be taken with great skepticism. In 1970 the NAS report found modified starches to be used for economic reasons. It found that some indication existed that the modified starches were not as digestible for infants under six months than other starches and that not enough evidence existed to conclusively resolve the question of digestibility.

Since 1970 the baby food industry has not seen fit to undertake any studies to resolve these questions. In addition, new questions about the imbalance of the nutrient to caloric ratio because of modified starches and the use of new untested modified starches have been raised.

The modified starch controversy remains unresolved. The baby food companies seem content to ignore it. That is a sure sign that parents should avoid the product.

SUGAR

Sugar is another controversial substance added to manufactured baby food. By merely tasting them, a parent may discover that a substantial portion of the calories in strained vegetables, for example, comes from sugar. The presence of sugar is an unfortunate counter to the advice of pediatricians that sugar should not be added to milk. The practice of adding sugar to infant foods has been attacked because it conditions the baby to eating "empty calories." Sugar is nutritionally poor, leads to poor dental health, and may even be related to heart disease. One of the most important aspects of good nutrition for pregnant women, infants and their families is the minimizing of sugar consumption.

In 1976 Gerber stated on the back of its cereal boxes that "nearly half of all Gerber baby foods contain no added sugar." The best answer to this argument is to avoid buying the other half (and buy this half only if it is free of MSG, HVP, salt and modified starches). Gerber also states flatly that the sugar content of its sugared foods is less than that of corresponding adult foods.

No evidence is provided for the claim and it refuses to list the sugar content on the product. In fact, for most baby foods which contain added sugar, such as fruits and juices, there exists an adult counterpart with no sugar added.

Gerber dismisses the problem of sugar by arguing that, "Cavities are not created by sugar, but are the action of bacteria growing in plaque on the surface of the teeth. These bacterial plaques may or may not be augmented by sugar, depending on a number of other factors."[27] The National Institute of Dental Research, one of the National Institutes of Health, describes the process somewhat differently. "Sweets should be restricted because any bacteria in the mouth uses sugar as the raw material to produce acid which dissolves tooth enamel. Sugar is also used by certain types of bacteria to manufacture a glue-like substance which enables them to stick to the tooth in a thin film called plaque. Held fast against the tooth, the bacteria bathe it in decay-producing acid."[28] The Institute warning about sugar is not directed to infants. However, an overly sweet diet in early life trains a child to eat sweet foods. As the Gerber Company points out, food fed to infants affects "life-long eating habits."[29] One of the habits nutritionists wish to avoid is the overfeeding of sugar. Overly sugared infant foods can lead to an excess of sugar in the diet of later life.

It is best to shop carefully and avoid sugared baby foods remembering that dextrose is also a type of sugar. Watch out for products which have both added sugar and added dextrose. These points hold true for all brands, not just Gerber products.

In addition, remember that sugar is concealed in other products which you might be buying for the rest of your family and giving to the baby as he or she grows old enough to eat from the table. Remember, never feed your child soft drinks in any form and in general do not serve sweet desserts daily or give your children sweet things as rewards. Save them for very special occasions. They should never be served as snacks or to shut up a noisy baby.

BEECH-NUT ANNOUNCEMENT

Some positive steps are being taken by the industry. As we were going to press, Beech-Nut Baby Foods announced they were introducing a line of baby foods free of salt, preservatives, artificial flavors and colors, and flavor enhancers. They also stated that 84 of their items would no longer contain any sugar at all and any item which did would contain no more than nine percent. They did not make mention of modified starch and their decision as to its use in baby foods. A shopper would be wise to keep an eye out for its inclusion in any baby food purchase.

The food industry is in a state of technological flux which requires the greatest degree of caution from food consumers and manufacturers alike. Dr. Jean Mayer spoke for many, both inside and outside the food industry, when he said, "I am growing uneasy about the progressive changes which new methods of food processing and food packaging are introducing into our nutrition. Nowhere are those changes more critical than in baby food."[30]

POINTS TO REMEMBER

The products which contribute most to the economic strength of the industry are the custards and puddings, fruits, meats, combinations and vegetables. These are often the ones which require the addition of the most starch and flavor enhancers. That baby food companies consciously develop products for economic purposes should cause all mothers to wonder how much "separate consideration" is given to baby food products. One good rule of thumb: if any baby foods are used, be sure they are not the more complex products. These tend to cost more and offer less.

A second good rule: Be prepared to discuss the

problem of solid feeding with your pediatrician on regular visits. It is widely accepted that early feeding of solids—before four to six months—is nutritionally unnecessary. Milk provides the needed nutrients during the early months. Discuss the articles on infant feeding cited above with the pediatrician. See what he or she thinks.

When Dr. Roger Williams of the University of Texas calls for expert consultation on nutritional needs he is emphasizing that professionals knowledgeable about nutrition—whether they are doctors or nutritionists—must learn to evaluate the nutritional needs of individuals and outline the best way to meet those needs. This is the strategy of the Montreal Dietary Clinic which has had such success in overcoming the nutritional deficiencies of the pregnant women who come to it. Nutritionally well-informed individuals can begin to provide that kind of counseling for themselves. Since there are few nutritional experts offering individual counseling today, personal knowledge may be the only way to provide for individual needs. Mothers and fathers should examine the basis of the processed baby food fad—and every other fad—to determine what value it provides. And they should remember that solid foods are not really necessary until four to six months at the earliest, and by that time foods from the table properly prepared can provide for the baby as well as the adults.

In examining processed baby foods, parents should compare their cost in both money and in convenience with other ways of feeding babies.

Finally parents must learn that the information

on baby food labels may not be the information needed to learn the value of the food inside. The labels do not say how much salt is added to the products, for example, though excess salt in baby foods has been criticized by the National Academy of Sciences. The FDA has proposed new regulations that require a complete label listing of each ingredient by its common name and its source. The proposed new regulations would require warnings on infant formula, where necessary, that a baby might require quantities of Vitamin C, Vitamin D, and iron in addition to those listed on the baby food jar. (See the Appendix for the complete text of the proposed FDA labeling regulations.)

It is just now becoming apparent that many assumptions about nutrition which have been held for years are not sound. Specifically, there is much that infants need that may not be in processed baby food. As of now there is no real way to tell. And as of now there are measurable dietary deficiencies affecting infants. This is a cause for national concern. A nation in which nearly every infant has an iron deficiency is not feeding its infants properly. That is why we must all become interested. We must work for the proper nutrition of our children. No longer can we feel secure in accepting the easy convenience of processed baby food.

PART III
THE ALTERNATIVES

BREASTFEEDING

Although there are no hard and fast figures for the number of women who breastfeed, nor are we able to separate these women into groups according to the length of time they nurse each baby, many more appear to be breastfeeding in recent years. The La Leche League, organized to help women breastfeed and to give them the kind of support which used to come from family and friends, has been growing by leaps and bounds. In 1960 the United States League contained only 16 groups (each group had between five and 15 members) and by 1968 there were 553. In 1972 there were 1,302 groups and by 1976 the number had jumped to 2,347. In our experience, the groups are quite large because many people who belong tell their friends. It becomes a way to meet new people, as well as obtain aid and comfort.

Whether to breastfeed or not is the first choice parents make concerning their child's nutrition. Despite the general recognition that breastfeeding is the natural and pleasant way to begin the relationship, it is estimated that three out of four babies born in the United States are completely bottlefed by the time they leave the hospital.

This low degree of commitment happens despite baby food companies' protestations that they produce only supplements. It happens despite the

Classes in natural childbirth preparation are extremely helpful and important. We feel they are essential for every new parent (husbands included) whether or not you go through with natural childbirth in the end. The information shared in class, the proper exercises taught, the contact with the teacher and with other expectant parents is very reassuring. Often you make new and lasting friendships with the people you meet. Contact the national offices listed below for the telephone number of your local chapter or for suggestions on how to start one if your area does not have one yet.

International Childbirth Education Association
P.O. Box 5852
Milwaukee, Wisconsin 53220

American Society for Psychoprophylaxis in Obstetrics
7 West 96th Street
New York, New York 10025

For the address and phone number of the La Leche League chapter closest to you, contact:
La Leche League International, Inc.
9616 Minneapolis Avenue
Franklin Park, Illinois 60131
(312) 455–7730

fact that many mothers begin life with their infant intending to breastfeed (in one study 68 percent of the mothers began breastfeeding but only 25 percent continued as long as two months). This occurs despite the fact that a growing group of prominent women and a number of leading physicians urge breastfeeding as the best, easiest and least expensive method of feeding infants.

Dr. David Reuben, who has gained some notice because of his writing on questions of sex, offers a number of strong reasons for breastfeeding. "Considered strictly from the standpoint of nutrition, babies fed on mother's milk tend to have more resistance to disease, lower incidence of colic, faster weight gain (though formula fed infants catch up later on), and a dozen or so other well-documented advantages in the early years of life."[1] Dr. Reuben also points out that nursing tends to make breasts firmer and more compact once lactation stops and that nursing a baby may provide substantial protection against breast cancer.

Doctors Spock and Lowenberg, who encourage nursing, point out that a nursing baby takes 1,000 calories of milk. This makes a comparable increase in dietary intake of the nursing mother necessary. Therefore, they suggest increasing daily intake of milk to six (eight ounce) glasses, meat (including liver) to between one quarter and one third of a pound, eggs to two and cereals by an extra serving. Fruit and vegetable servings can remain the same as during pregnancy. To avoid allergic reactions, a possibility when drinking large quantities of milk, be sure to first heat the milk to a hot, not boiling, temperature. Also we suggest, if the idea of drinking such enormous quantities of milk is unappealing, you see the other acceptable liquids we have included in our variation of the Spock-Lowenberg prenatal diet in the chapter entitled "The Prenatal Diet."

Healthier and easier, breastfeeding also performs an important psychological function. Dr. Margaret Ribble, in her book *The Rights of Infants,* places breastfeeding near the top on her list of rights. Beginning infant feeding with the bottle is possible, she says, if "the immediate sense of security which breastfeeding brings to the infant, from close contact and being held securely, is given it at the same time. But it is makeshift at best and never to the child's advantage."[2] Dr. Ribble's studies led her to conclude that bottlefed babies must be regarded as deprived individuals unless the parents succeed in showing love through other forms of attention.

Since 1972 nutritionists and doctors have developed and presented more extensive information on breastfeeding. In 1975 Dr. Betty J. Oseid wrote a detailed review of current information on the subject. She began by saying, "Breastfeeding well into the second or third year, either by the mother or a wet nurse, had been the usual mode of feeding infants until the twentieth century."[3]

In recent years, however, a number of food processing techniques have led to the development of manufactured infant formula. For certain infants, such as those whose mothers suffer from active tuberculosis, or who have had radical mastectomies, this technology offers a useful alternative. For the normal healthy infant, however, the manufactured formula alternative adds nothing.

The American Academy of Pediatrics sets out Standards and Recommendations for Hospital Care of Newborn Infants. On breastfeeding it states: "Breastfeeding is recommended for all full-term and vigorous preterm infants because human milk is nutritionally sound and because breastfeeding tends to facilitate a close mother-child relationship."[4]

Dr. Oseid sets out a series of reasons for the superiority of breastfeeding. Human milk offers measurable nutritional superiority over formula. It offers protection against infectious diseases. Reliance on breastfeeding alone gives a probable advantage to infants predisposed to allergy, ulcerative colitis and celiac disease. Ear infections, gross bacterial contamination and lead ingestion are less likely in breastfed infants. Breastfeeding provides a mother the maximum opportunity to develop attachment to the infant, it stimulates infant sensor perception and develops basic trust through spreading of pleasurable feelings. Dr. Oseid also lists breastfeeding as a possible form of contraception which many people feel presents still another advantage. That is not to say that it works for all women, but scientists know it does in fact slow down the birth rate. Finally, she points out that breastfeeding is "convenient, hygienic, time saving and economical."[5]

As if all of this were not enough, it has also been discovered by a number of doctors that bottlefeeding leads to tooth decay in a number of children. Putting a child to bed with a bottle of juice, formula or milk allows the sugar liquid to dribble onto the teeth all night and cause decay. A more detailed look at the various reasons for breastfeeding might help in making up your mind.

NUTRITIONAL ADVANTAGES OF HUMAN MILK

Dr. D. B. Jelliffe, Professor of Public Health and Pediatrics at UCLA, asked the fundamental question in a 1975 article. "Can cow's milk formula ever in fact in any way approximate human milk?" He also provided his own answer. "This seems a total impossibility. . . ."[6]

There are more than one hundred components in human milk. The fatty acid content of human milk is totally different from that in cow's milk. It is this fact that gives the breastfed infant a potential advantage in preventing excessive production of undesirable cholesterol later on in childhood or adulthood, according to some researchers.

Human milk is a living fluid like blood. Each mother's milk is a specific for her child. It contains living cells and active enzymes which aid in the digestion of the milk's nutritional components. This quality cannot be duplicated by manufacturing techniques currently known. As a result some researchers feel that human milk gives the infant an advantage. It is also sterile and always at a constant temperature.

The human infant brain grows at an extraordinarily rapid pace. Some researchers now believe that the high amounts of certain nutrients, such as lactose and linoleic acid present in human milk as compared to cow's milk, probably are an essential contributing factor to optimum infant brain development during this period of rapid growth.

Mineral balance in human milk appears to be superior to available alternatives. In this case the level in human milk for a number of essential minerals is about one third of that in cow's milk. This offers an important advantage to the breastfed infant. Since human milk provides an adequate number of minerals in most cases and does not require the elimination of excessive amounts, the load placed on the immature infant kidney system is significantly reduced.

One mineral, iron, is not present in human milk in adequate amounts. Some doctors recommend supplementation during breastfeeding for the first six months. Others argue that waiting until the baby is six months old and feeding it meats and cereals which contain iron will be adequate. While cow's milk has more iron than human milk, it is a form that may not be well-absorbed by the infant. This is an issue to discuss with your doctor. You might also want to discuss it with your local La Leche League chapter and review the available literature.

If mothers pay attention to their diets and eat well-balanced meals, their breast milk will provide acceptable levels of vitamin A, thiamine, riboflavin, niacin, B_6, B_{12}, folic acid, and vitamins C and E.

Vitamin D is a different and more complicated story. Each infant needs vitamin D supplements.

Each infant must be protected from excessive amounts of vitamin D which can be dangerous. Excessive amounts can cause hypercalcemia, a condition which in severe forms involves changes in the bony structure of the face, affects the arteries of the heart and causes mental retardation.

The National Academy of Sciences has established 300 to 400 International Units (IUs) of vitamin D as the safe level for infants and for adults. It is important to be sure that this amount is not exceeded. Supplements will be labeled in the amount of IUs per serving. Check the labels *on all products* fed to your infant to be sure that vitamin D from different sources does not exceed 400 IUs per day. And remember, all supplements should be discussed with your physician.

New manufactured cow's milk-based formulas have attempted to match human milk and are closer to it than evaporated milk-based formulas, but they run up against the impossibility of matching the known nutritional qualities of breast milk.

As your baby grows older and becomes interested in food he or she will lose interest in the breast and will wean his or herself. You do not have to wean your baby to a bottle; by weaning time the baby should, with some help, be able to use a cup. Let the baby have a say in determining when it is ready to quit.

DISEASE PREVENTING ADVANTAGES OF HUMAN MILK

Breastfeeding has known disease-preventing advantages. It contains protective antibodies against more than a dozen disease-causing viruses, in addition to polio, and including salmonella and influenza. It also contains organisms which inhibit the development of diseases such as septicemia and meningitis in newborns. A number of studies in animals and in the treatment for some newly emerging diseases, particularly in premature infants who suffer severe perinatal stress, suggests new areas of possible disease prevention related to the consumption of human milk.

In addition to lessened susceptibility to infectious diseases caused by viruses, and digestive track diseases, breastfed infants also have a lower incidence of middle ear infections. These infections apparently occur because bottlefed babies are often left lying on their backs with propped bottles. If you do decide to bottlefeed or supplement, remember: always hold your baby; *never prop the bottle*. The disease-preventing aspects of human milk, like its nutritional factors, cannot be reproduced by food technology. Since increasing evidence connecting breastfeeding with better infant health has begun to accumulate, a controversy about its significance has developed. Proponents of formula feeding argue that well-educated mothers, living in affluent societies and preparing their formula accurately according to directions, will get the same health benefits from formula as from breast milk. They argue that the correlation between bottlefeeding and sick and dying babies is confined to underdeveloped communities where clean water is a luxury and good food a rarity.

Dr. Jelliffe comments on this argument in a way each mother should be aware of. "Such host resistant factors." he wrote about the protective capability of breast milk, "plainly have more significance in countries where infections are common and the hygienic background is worse. But nevertheless they may have more importance in so-called developed countries than imagined. For instance, in Sweden it has been shown that babies who are breastfed from birth have a lower incidence of neonatal septicemia."[7]

Because most mothers who breastfeed do so for less than the minimum desirable six months, it is difficult to organize and carry out studies comparing the effects of various kinds of early feeding. What evidence there is suggests great disease protection advantages when one relies on breastfeeding.

CONTRACEPTION, CONVENIENCE AND COMPANIONSHIP OFFERED BY BREASTFEEDING

Breastfeeding, folk wisdom said, led to natural contraception, better spacing of children and therefore a happier, more orderly family life. For years "the experts" chuckled at this old wives' tale. With a psychological, if not an actual, pat on the head, modern doctors chided mothers about the easy spread of such ignorance and sent them on their way.

Now more careful study by researchers supports the wives' tale. Dr. Jelliffe says, "In the last few years work has shown very clearly that successful unsupplemented lactation has a definite contraceptive effect lasting for months, which declines with the introduction of supplements and with time."[8] A word of warning: The contraceptive effect does not operate the same way for all mothers, so do not count on it if you want to be certain of the spacing of your children. It works well for some women and not at all for others, but it is no longer a myth.

Recent work on the cost and convenience of breastfeeding has also punctured an old myth. It had been argued by some that cow's milk cost less and was easier to use nutritionally. This argument rested on the assumption that women would need to consume a richer, more costly diet to make adequate breast milk.

It turns out that low cost, nutritionally adequate foods available to mothers can produce enough nutritionally superior breast milk to make cow's milk a costly and inconvenient food. Alan Berg, of the World Bank, has estimated that the cost of ignoring breast milk world-wide exceeds $50 billion annually.

In addition to all its other benefits, breastfeeding builds the relationship between mother and infant. Closeness to the heart beat of the mother, de-

velopment of maternal attachment, a basic sense of
trust, rapid satisfaction of hunger needs, all flow
from the breastfeeding relationship between mothers
and infants. All have been documented by researchers. Mothers, not only infants, need the continua-
tion of closeness that they have had for the nine
months previous to birth. Separation is psychologically bad for both.

One study showed that the closeness of mothers
to their infants immediately following birth and
throughout their hospital stay led to more fondling of
the infants, more soothing behavior from the mother
toward the child, more direct face to face contact
between the infant and the mother and a greater re-
luctance on the part of the mother to leave the infant
to another's care. Two years after the birth, the
mothers with the greater contact had better and more
complex language interaction and tended to use
questions rather than commands in modifying their
babies' behavior.

To some extent this closeness can be ac-
complished with a bottlefed baby. It takes a conscientious effort to make sure the bottle is ready
when the baby cries, that the bottle is never propped,
that the baby is not left with other people before the
baby is ready. Breastfeeding mothers take their
babies with them, rather than leave them with a sit-
ter. Then when the baby is hungry, it is not necessary to rush home to feed it or to start fiddling with
heating bottles. Nature has built in a marvelous system for keeping a mother close to the tiny baby who
needs to be held and fed. But if it is necessary for
you to bottlefeed, remember to make the extra effort

at being close to your baby. Steps to achieve this closeness are at the end of this chapter. It is possible; in the study described above the babies were bottlefed.[9]

PROMOTING BOTTLEFEEDING

We believe the situation is such in the baby food industry that you cannot depend on its products to provide you with the best possible nutrition for your infant at the fairest price and with as much safety as possible.

The activity of the baby formula companies, particularly on the international scene, underlines this argument with stark and unpleasant statistics. Cornell University Nutritionist, Professor Michael Latham and his associate Ted Greiner revealed a short study in February, 1976 in which they argued that bottlefeeding is one of the prime contributory factors in the high rate of infant mortality in developing nations.

"For two thirds of the world's population," the two nutritionists wrote, "bottlefeeding of infants is highly undesirable. In many instances, placing an infant on a bottle is tantamount to signing the death certificate of the child."[10]

The Cornell study suggests that advertising by the large infant formula companies, Gerber, Nestlé, Bristol-Myers, Borden, the makers of Beech-Nut Baby Food and many others, is possibly the single most important reason for the spread of bottlefeeding. The companies' annual reports make clear how proud they are of their formula selling campaigns.

Latham and Greiner write that "Advertisements imply that nice people with nice houses who want nice babies, bottlefeed their babies . . . the medical onslaught is terrific, the messages are powerful, and the profits are high. High also is the resultant human suffering. . . ."[11]

The study described "diaper derbies" in underdeveloped countries featuring crawling contests, the use of clowns, magicians and circus performers and the enlisting of nurses and doctors, as well as extensive and misleading advertising campaigns— all designed to promote the sales of formula. This onslaught, the authors feel, has caused a major portion of the deadly shift away from breastfeeding. Deadly because in developing nations there is little refrigeration or modern water supplies. Babies are left at home while mothers travel to the city to work and the formula is mixed by small children charged with taking care of the baby. The water used is not sterile, the bottles are not clean, there is no refrigeration, and worst of all, the powdered formula is diluted because the families cannot afford to buy as much as they should for the baby. Thus, the infant literally starves to death, if it is not killed first by an intestinal infection.

The Cornell researchers say that Americans need not fear this problem because bottlefeeding in this country when done properly is not dangerous. But here in the United States we have our share of people who live in conditions not so unlike some of the less-developed nations. The children born to America's poor surely suffer nutritionally when not offered a breast milk beginning in life.

As pointed out earlier, individuals like Doctors Jelliffe and Oseid, and the scientists whose work they use in researching their published papers, indicate that breastfed babies may be healthier. No one argues convincingly that bottle babies are healthier.

A HAPPIER NOTE

Occasionally breastfeeding a newborn infant is not possible. If you have adopted your baby or you are unable to nurse because of health problems do not despair. Here are a few suggestions to help you make it a pleasant experience for both you and your baby.

1. Always hold your baby while it is feeding. Never leave an infant propped up on a pillow with a bottle.

2. Sit in a comfortable chair with a pillow at your neck or back. If possible, a high-backed rocker is preferable.

3. Remember to switch the baby from one arm to the other in the middle of the feeding, just as you would if you were breastfeeding.

4. Try to find a formula which does not contain sugar. Be sure to consult your doctor before making a decision.

5. Try to approximate body temperature (98.6°) when heating the bottle. The formula does not have to be hot but it should not be ice cold.

6. Your baby knows you by your smell and touch and heartbeat. One of the nicest things about breastfeeding is holding the baby against your skin.

If you bottlefeed you can still hold the baby against your naked breast and not miss out on this pleasurable experience.

Of course, unless it is absolutely necessary to bottlefeed, we strongly suggest you choose to breastfeed. Let Dr. Jelliffe sum it up:

> The time has come to realize that breastfeeding and human milk embody the latest scientific advances in modern nutrition, in infant feeding, and in child-rearing. More than any other example, breastfeeding exemplifies the need to incorporate both biological considerations and traditional background into the technological "future shock" world that is increasingly upon us.[12]

Breastfeeding uses food supplies efficiently, presents an ecologically-biologically balanced feeding system and conserves energy. You get all these benefits and a happier family.

FROM MILK
TO SOLIDS

Once an infant reaches the age of four to six months and shows an interest in trying new foods, it is time to introduce it to solid foods. Dr. Margaret Ribble points out three discoveries made by infants which eventually lead to this natural weaning—the need for varied food, infant awareness of its own voice, and the distinction between mother and food. As these discoveries develop into a general awareness the natural interest of the infant, her studies show, shifts from the sucking of breast milk to the eating of food.

Going from a diet made up entirely of milk to one which includes a few solids is an important step in an infant's life. Some societies mark it with ceremonial rites of passage because it is so important. Nutritionists indicate several considerations that should accompany the gradual transition:

(1) Food should be nutritious.

(2) It should be acceptable to the infant and its family.

(3) It should be possible to prepare without excessive effort.

(4) It should be clean and prepared in clean surroundings.

The weaning process, of course, is not an abrupt one. It should be helped along by the gradual introduction of food into the baby's diet along with milk. Each of the steps in changing the diet can be taken with the guidance of a physician to dispel any doubts and answer questions as they come up. In fact, many babies today are allowed to nurse if only once a day until age two. (They are also, by this time, eating three meals a day and discovering many new foods.)

In keeping with the fact that infant feeding serves more than a nutritional purpose, the shift from a milk-only to a milk and pure supplements diet should be made when the infant is ready for new oral experiences. Dr. Ribble sets this time at about four or five months. A good measure for individual infants is the point at which they begin to sit up by themselves, to reach for or show some interest in feeding utensils, and make some effort to become involved in feeding themselves.

Any earlier feeding of solids could well lead to problems. Helen A. Guthrie, writing in *Pediatrics,* warns against the growing trend to feed solids to infants at earlier and earlier ages—some mothers were feeding solids by the end of the first month or even earlier. "Processors of special infant foods may well have stimulated the demand for such a feeding program."[1] For whatever reasons, early feeding of solids gained some acceptance. But there is no medical or scientific evidence to support the practice.

Early solid food feeding may increase suscepti- bility to allergies, and it may cause the kidneys to work excessively. The frustrations of mothers trying to feed solids to infants unable to eat or digest them, may cause unhappy feelings to be attached to eating. Some researchers feel that too early feeding may lead to frustration. In addition there is no nutritional purpose served by feeding early. As one researcher put it, the practice of early feeding of solids is "unphysiologic, time consuming and unnecessarily expensive."[2]

As your child reaches four or five months, and the doctor is urging you to begin solids, there are a number of factors to keep in mind. What follows are some specific alternatives and suggested recipes for making your own baby food.

DOING YOUR OWN THING

Feeding your baby yourself can be far simpler than running to the store and picking out different kinds of cereals, fruits, vegetables, and meat dishes, as some doctors suggest each time you go to see them. Pediatricians, who often rely on promotional material provided to them by the baby food industry, tend to stress variety and the necessity of introducing your child to different kinds of fruits or vegetables. It is not necessary to do this. A growing number of people are feeding their children homemade baby food of a much simpler kind and finding that as the children grow up, they branch out to other kinds of foods.

The young baby and child are not known for their discriminating desire for gourmet foods. So in a very real sense you are just wasting your time by purchasing all the different recommended foods. Our parents and grandparents did not eat food until they were able to sit up at the table and nibble at small bits of food from a parent's plate. Nature has provided a unique and perfect infant feeding system and all man has tried to do is improve on it, often to his further discomfort and expense. Formerly, babies were nursed until about one year or so, when the arrival of teeth enabled them to chew.

Keeping this in mind, you will learn in the pages ahead a number of simple recipes for baby food which parents are now using in their attempts to give their children more nutritious meals.

Initially, making your own baby food involves a bit more effort on your part because you will have to acquire a few additional supplies, read a few more books than you might have planned, shop carefully until you get the knack of it, and think about what you are going to put inside your child. But this is part of your responsibility as a parent in any case.

You will want to think of new foods, find new stores, and try out different ways of making and storing food. What follows is merely a suggested list. One of the joys of homemade baby food is that you improvise and create according to your and your baby's desires.

SUPPLIES

A good food blender is a necessity. This item can run as high as $50 or as low as $20, depending on where you get it. As an appliance it should last a

long time and it will be used for many things besides
baby food—most blenders come with recipe books
for intriguing new concoctions. Try to get a blender
that comes with mini-jar attachments. They are very
handy when it comes to making baby food.

Many parents have also found a table-model
food grinder to be most useful. The food can be
ground immediately after cooking and served to
baby. Consistency can be changed by adding more
liquid. It makes about a cup of food at a time and can
be purchased in some supermarkets and department
stores. (The Happy Baby Food Grinder, Bowland-
Jacobs Manufacturing Co., 8 Oakdale Rd., Spring
Valley, Ill. 61362 is excellent.)

Mini-blender jars for mixing small quantities
and for storage are very useful.

A thermos jar is important for carrying an infant's meal when going for a day's outing and you
want to keep the meal warm.

Any of the recipes can easily be carried in a
thermos or in regular screwtop jars stuffed into a
corner of a plasticized diaper bag if the meal is good
cold. For example, a frozen cube of stew will thaw
by the time you get to a restaurant or to someone
else's house. (Also, babies do not seem to care
whether food is heated, cool or lukewarm. Remember, their taste buds just have not progressed
that far.) If you haven't got far to travel, defrost the
cube in advance so it is not still icy when you arrive
at your destination.

By only having to carry one kind of food for
your baby, you also eliminate all that fussing with
several jars of food.

A freezer compartment in your refrigerator is essential for storing baby food for periods of time without loss of food value and freshness. And it is always time saving to make an extra batch to freeze and store. Plastic ice cube trays, the kind you simply pop out one cube at a time, can simplify storage of food for infants. By freezing the blended food in cube-sized portions, you will save yourself valuable time. When it is time to feed baby, you just remove a portion, heat it up and serve.

SHOPPING

Initially you will have to spend more time shopping carefully for wholesome nutritious foods for your family. But once you discover where the good stores are in your vicinity, when they get fresh produce and eggs in, and where to buy special products for less than in the health food stores, you will find shopping and preparing meals for your baby and family much simpler and quicker and you can relax knowing that they are eating well.

In addition, one of the bonuses is that your children will not be up at all hours of the night suffering from runny noses, empty stomachs, sore gums, etc. The parents who spend the time shopping and preparing healthy foods for their children are rewarded with more time to play with and enjoy their beautifully strong and happy offspring.

Visit a number of supermarkets to find out which ones carry really fresh produce, which have a butcher who will cut up meat especially for you, and otherwise seem to cater to the tastes of their customers. Compare the color of meat in various stores. Generally, the redder it is, the better it is. But not always.

Visit all the health food stores within reasonable distance from your house. Compare prices of staple items such as eggs, soy margarine, butter, fresh bread, all fresh organic produce and cold-pressed oils. Then decide whether you can use a store closer to you for perishables while making a monthly trip to the best health food store for special things like hot dogs free of all additives (serve these as a special treat for your children), large boxes of carob powder, whole powdered milk (to use in making puddings and soups), large containers of chewable natural vitamin C tablets, etc.

Investigate small specialty stores run by people interested in wholesome foods. Perhaps there is a local farmer who grows organic vegetables, or a man who raises bees and will sell you "real," as opposed to watered down, honey. These small stores often carry such items as homemade bread (which can be frozen and re-frozen), rolls, hot dog buns, unadulterated peanut butter, fresh maple syrup and eggs from fresh free-range (not caged) chickens.

You must learn to read the label on any new product you buy. Once you know which items to include and which to exclude, your shopping becomes infinitely easier. In general, you can be suspicious of all new products, those advertised on television or in magazines, and those in flashy boxes. Any convenience, pre-cooked, pre-packaged foods, as well as TV dinners, etc., are *out*.

THE
RECIPES

When you begin feeding your baby solids, the easiest things to feed him or her are bananas, egg yolks and yogurt. Following are several suggestions for easy recipes. The quantities and ingredients can be varied at will. Baby food is not like making a cake; if you put in too much banana, it will not fall flat. The recipes are listed in the order in which you might try them, starting with foods for four to six month old babies, and continuing with suggestions for feeding older children and the rest of the family.

BASIC FOODS

BANANA

Banana makes an excellent first food for your baby and is easy to carry if you travel or go out to dinner.

1 *ripe banana*

Peel the banana (the browner the skin, the better) and mash it in a dish with a fork. You can serve it plain as your baby's introduction to solids and then later mix it with other foods. Some of the things you may wish to mix with the banana include a bit of milk, cereal, brewer's yeast (if your family tolerates it try your baby on ¼ teaspoon per banana), yogurt and other fruits, raw and blended.

COOKED EGG YOLK

1 *egg, raw*
Apple juice or milk

Place the unshelled egg in a saucepan and cover with cold water. Bring to a boil over medium heat and immediately reduce the flame or the eggshell will crack. Simmer for 20 minutes.

When the egg is done place the pan under cold running water to cool. Let the egg sit in cold water for 15 minutes. When it is cold it can be easily cracked. Peel, and place only the yolk in a small dish for the baby. Make sure you do not include any of the white part. Add some apple juice or milk to moisten (some mothers use breast milk which they have expressed). Make sure it is moist enough— almost liquid for a small baby. Serve a little at a time giving just a few tastes at first. If allergic, he or she may throw up soon after the egg reaches the stomach. If your baby likes the egg you could try adding a bit of banana.

YOGURT

Yogurt seems to be just about the perfect beginning food for babies. It contains bacteria which help the baby's stomach to produce the valuable B vitamins which he or she needs for growth. Plain unflavored yogurt to which you can add fruit or other things, is the healthiest. It contains no sugar. Select a brand that has no additives and use it as a basic food, much as you do the banana. Because babies do not have the highly developed aesthetic sense about foods that their parents have they do not seem to mind foods mixed together.

Since yogurt is not sweet, it is a good idea to accustom your child to eating it every day before the baby gets too familiar with sweet commercial foods. Yogurt travels well and does not spoil easily. When traveling, put a thermos container into the freezer to insure maximum coldness, and then fill it with plain yogurt. As you travel you can remove as much as you need. Add half a mashed banana or any mashed ripe fruit which you have brought along.

Note: Making your own yogurt is cheap and easy. You can now buy an electric yogurt-maker which makes the process even easier.

BEYOND THE BASICS

OTHER FRESH FRUITS

Berries and other fruits in season are excellent for babies and small children. Try to buy them fresh from a local farm stand if possible. Make sure you wash and drain the fruit well before serving it to the baby. We have tried the following with great success.

Strawberries. Remove stems and mash with a fork until soft.

Blueberries. Try just a few mashed in yogurt.

Peaches. Peel, and if very ripe, mash with a fork.

Apples. Peel and slice. Purée in a blender with a bit of apple juice. Makes a lovely applesauce.

Pears. Peel, slice and mash with a fork.

Remember, some babies gag easily. Our children were not gaggers and could manage whole blueberries and strawberries as finger food at about eight months old. If your baby gags, wait several months before giving blueberries or small-sized pieces of any fruit.

Since we are talking of gagging, here might be a good place to mention that you should *never give your baby or toddler whole corn, peas, or peanuts.* They are a perfect size to fill a small windpipe and each year there are children who choke to death on them.

CEREALS

There is some dispute about the necessity of giving infants cereals almost immediately. If you are nursing and eating well yourself, your baby should not need a supplement. Cereals are designed to fill up baby's stomach while providing very little nourishment. Familia® Swiss cereal makes a finely ground cereal for infants. When you start feeding your baby yogurt and fruit you can add this cereal. Serve it after baby has had yogurt mixture. Do not feel that it is necessary to stuff your baby full of cereal as you will see so many others doing.

COTTAGE CHEESE OR TAPIOCA FRUIT

Cottage Cheese Fruit

> ½ cup cottage cheese without salt if pos-
>   sible
> ½ cup fresh fruit, raw
> 4 to 6 tablespoons apple juice depending
>   on the desired consistency

Tapioca Fruit

> ½ cup cooked tapioca (use the recipe for
>   Honey Tapioca in this book)
> ½ cup fresh fruit, raw

With each of these recipes, put contents into a mini-blender jar, if possible, and blend at low speed until smooth. Either mixture may be stored in the refrigerator for a few days. (Bananas do not keep as well as other fruits.)

VEGETABLES

FIRST VEGETABLES

Eventually you will want to introduce your child to vegetables. It is best to start with a bland one like acorn squash or sweet potato.

1 *acorn squash, sweet potato or yam*
  Apple juice

Any of these three vegetables can be baked in a hot (425°) oven for 45 minutes, or until done. Remove and allow to cool down. Then scoop out the squash or potato from its skin and mash. Add a little apple juice for extra taste and a smoother consistency. Serve this at room temperature. Leftovers can be stored in the refrigerator for a few days.

Once your baby is enjoying these mild-flavored vegetables, offer peas, spinach, white potatoes, carrots or beets. These should all be bought fresh from the market, steamed first and then either mashed or blended. A white potato may be baked in its skin rather then steamed.

VEGETABLE PURÉE

Some vegetables seem to go well together, others do not. You might try a purée of carrots and white potato for a start.

½ *cup steamed carrots*
½ *cup steamed white potato*
  Milk

Put both the potato and the carrots into a blender jar. Add a little milk for consistency and blend until smooth.

If your child likes this combination try adding another vegetable—steamed celery or green beans go nicely. You can add and subtract to suit the season and the baby's personal taste.

MEATS

A small amount of boiled beef in plenty of broth or cooking liquid is a nice way to get a baby going on meat.

BOILED BEEF

> 1 *cup stewing beef (chuck is fine) cubed and with all the fat removed*
> 1 *cup fresh beef broth or stock, or liquid reserved from cooking vegetables*

In a heavy saucepan combine the beef and cooking liquid. Bring to a boil over medium heat, then reduce flame so that the liquid is just simmering. Cover the pot and allow the meat to cook slowly until tender. This may take one hour or less depending on the size of the meat cubes. Add water to the pot if the liquid cooks down.

When done, cool to room temperature. Pour the cooking liquid into a blender, add a few of the meat cubes and blend until the mixture is puréed. Keep adding meat cubes until the mixture is a loose but pleasant consistency. Keep in mind that babies like meat very moist, so pleasant to them means nice and juicy.

MEAT STEWS

After your baby has become accustomed to meat and vegetables, introduce him or her to an easy-to-make, nourishing stew. It is puréed and easy to digest.

Beef Stew

1 *cup stewing beef cubed and with all the fat removed*

¼ *cup diced carrots, green beans, peas, spinach or any vegetable your baby favors*

¼ *cup potato, white, sweet or yam, peeled and diced*

½ *cup liquid (stock, water or milk or a combination of any of them)*

Liver or Lamb Stew

1 *cup beef liver or lamb (cut from the shoulder or leg) cubed and with all the fat removed*

1 *tablespoon onion, chopped (this can be omitted if the baby does not like the taste)*

½ *cup beef broth or stock from cooking*

¼ *cup milk*

¼ *cup potato, peeled and diced*

Chicken-and-Rice Stew

1 *cup chicken, cubed*

¼ *cup brown rice*

¼ *cup vegetable, diced (see Beef Stew for suggestions)*

½ *cup chicken broth or stock*

½ *cup milk*

For all three recipes, combine ingredients in a heavy saucepan and bring to a boil over medium heat. Reduce the flame so that stew is just simmering.

Cover the pan and cook until meat is tender. Check occasionally to make sure the cooking liquid has not evaporated. Add more liquid as needed.

Cooking time differs for these stews, beef and lamb taking longer than the chicken or liver. If you make the meat cubes tiny, cooking time will lessen. If you do not want to overcook the vegetables add them to the pan after the meat has cooked and seems nearly done—a half hour for chicken and liver, an hour for beef and lamb (more if the meat still seems tough).

When the stew is done, allow it to cool before putting it in the blender. Purée on a high speed with some of the cooking liquid. Reserve any liquid you do not need for a future date.

Any extra stew can be easily frozen in an ice cube tray (see Supplies in the chapter entitled "From Milk to Solids"). Once frozen, pop the stew cubes out and put them in a plastic bag in your freezer. The tray will then be empty and ready for use and you will have a convenient supply of stew cubes for your baby's dinners. Each of the above recipes fills one ice cube tray.

As your child grows and you become more adept at experimenting, just add to the blender whatever you are having for dinner and make instant puréed food for your baby. The baby needs no seasonings in its food so perhaps you can cook without seasonings, purée baby's portion, and then add salt, pepper and other favorites to the rest of your family's food upon serving.

Making puréed food this way takes approximately two extra minutes. For example, if you are serving steak and peas, just before you sit down to eat put some of both into the blender and purée for baby. Then you can all sit down to eat together.

As your baby's teeth appear, somewhere around one year of age, you can begin to give pieces of meat, potato and vegetable right off your plate. That is how our grandparents learned to eat at the table.

TEETHING FOODS

When your baby starts teething, instead of buying teething biscuits which consist only of carbohydrates and sugars, and which make a sloppy mess, try carrots, apples or celery. Beware of teething rings filled with liquid since occasionally they do break and release unsanitary fluid into your child's mouth.

BABY FOODS THE WHOLE FAMILY CAN EAT

Since we wrote this book we have added a daughter to our family. Victoria is now three years old; Chris, our son, is now 10.

We found that Victoria was more interested in eating at an earlier age than her brother had been and was willing to try anything he was eating. This meant that if he was eating something not suitable for an infant, we requested that he not eat it in her presence. It became a matter of planning and skill to prepare things which all of us could eat and enjoy.

Toddlers with few teeth, and smaller babies too, can sit at the table and benefit from the social experience if the food offered is mushy and does not require sharp teeth for chewing. A tasty cheese quiche (after you remove the crust for the baby's portion) can be elegant and edible. A mousse or cream soup can be eaten by all.

We have included in this new edition a number of recipes which friends have found over the years to be successful with all members of the family. These recipes were developed by exceedingly busy people who do not spend long hours in the kitchen, but who are interested in good nutrition for their families. Many of the recipes include a basic starter, simple and unseasoned, to which you add seasonings enjoyed by older members of the family. For example, in making the basic crepe recipe, leave out the salt initially and make several crepes for your small children, then add salt and make the rest for everyone else. (You may also find yourself leaving out the salt for older people and guests with hypertension.)

In making quiche, process pieces of ham in a blender rather than just chopping them. If you are feeding a number of children make a separate quiche just for them without salt and ham.

It is easier than you think and once you get started and feel comfortable, you can begin to experiment and add your own things. This book is meant to give you a start. As your child grows older, just substitute regular food for the puréed items.

Note: Small children often do not enjoy herbs and other seasonings. While we have, in most recipes, suggested seasonings to add for extra flavoring, they are not essential for the child's enjoyment. Therefore, we do not list them as part of the necessary ingredients.

AVOCADO SALAD

Avocados are very nutritious and many small children like them. They can be eaten plain or added to other things. We recommend one quarter to one half of an avocado for a baby and one whole one for two adults. Here are some suggestions.

For an infant. Mash ripe avocado in a small dish with a fork. Can be eaten with fingers or a small spoon as baby grows and learns how to use one.

For older children. Slice avocado on a plate and serve plain with a squeeze of fresh lemon or with small pieces of fresh orange or grapefruit.

For adults. Mix sliced avocado with sliced fresh grapefruit. Add a french dressing or Phil's Dressing (see below).

You can add more grapefruit if you want to stretch this dish. We use this on a bed of lettuce as a salad, as a dessert, or just eat it as a main dish on a hot summer day.

Avocados may also be added to fresh green salads for a delicious treat.

BLENDER MAYONNAISE

This is delicious on salads, particularly since it is made in small amounts and is usually fresh.

> 1 *egg, raw*
> ½ *teaspoon dry mustard*
> ¼ *teaspoon paprika*
> 1 *tablespoon vinegar*
> 1 *teaspoon lemon*
> 1 *cup safflower oil*
> ½ *teaspoon salt for adult portion*

Put the egg, mustard, paprika, vinegar, lemon and ¼ cup of the oil into a blender. Blend for a minute or two stopping to scrape down the sides with a rubber spatula if necessary.

Slowly add the rest of the oil through the hole in the lid. Continue blending until the mixture is thick.

Set aside a portion for the baby and add the salt to the remaining mayonnaise. Blend a few seconds more until salt is evenly mixed.

Store any you do not use in a glass jar in the refrigerator.

PHIL'S SALAD DRESSING SUPREME

Phil is Mary's 30 year old brother who has become a fantastic cook. As a child he ate only hamburgers, hot dogs and beans, peanut butter and bacon sandwiches. His mother thought he would die of malnutrition. Now, as a marine biologist, he dives for Jacques Cousteau off the ship Calypso and enjoys eating Madame Cousteau's scrumptious meals. So do not despair if your child does not eat. There is hope.

> ¾ *cup safflower oil*
> ¼ *cup wine vinegar*
> 1 *tablespoon honey (or more to taste)*
> 1 *clove fresh garlic, crushed*

Put all ingredients into a glass jar with a tight fitting lid and shake well. This is a basic dressing which is delicious on most salads.

If the older children and adult family members prefer a little salt, pepper and herbal flavoring in their dressing, set a portion aside for the younger children and add extra seasoning to the rest.

CHICKEN OR TURKEY STOCK

This stock is made without any added seasoning and is a good base to use in preparing soups, stews, vegetables or any other dishes calling for a cooking liquid.

> *Bones from a leftover chicken or turkey carcass*

Place the bones in a large pot and cover with water. Bring to a boil over a high flame and then lower to the simmering point. Skim off the top any scum which may have accumulated.

Simmer for four hours or until meat scraps fall off the bones easily. Strain the broth, reserving the meat for sandwiches or salads. The bones can go into the garbage.

Pour the stock into a plastic container with a lid and set in the refrigerator overnight. Before using skim the fat off the top.

This stock should be kept in the refrigerator for no longer than a week to 10 days.

CREAMY POTATO SOUP

This soup tastes good either hot or cold depending on the season.

> 3 *large potatoes, peeled and quartered*
> 1 *stalk celery or handful of celery leaves*
> 1 *medium-sized onion*
> ½ *cup chicken or turkey stock*
> ½ *cup milk*

Clean the vegetables and put them in a saucepan with enough water to cover and bring to a boil. Cook until just tender. Drain but reserve the cooking liquid.

Put the vegetables into a blender with a little of the liquid. Blend to a thick consistency.

Pour mixture into a heavy saucepan and add about a ½ cup of stock and a ½ cup of milk. Stir over a low flame. If you want a thinner soup add more stock. More milk will make it creamier.

Season the adult portion with crushed fresh garlic, chopped dill and ground pepper if you wish. Toasted bread croutons on the top taste lovely.

SPINACH SOUP

Make this the same way you make the Creamy Potato Soup substituting fresh or frozen chopped spinach for the potatoes. You will need one package or one pound. If you use fresh, make sure it is well-rinsed to remove any grit. Drain thoroughly.

Garnish with chopped hardboiled eggs and grated cheese.

CREAM SAUCE BASE FOR SOUPS

Our children always prefer a cream sauce soup to one made with stock.

   4 *tablespoons butter or use a light oil such as safflower*
   ¼ *cup whole-wheat flour*
   2 *cups heated milk*

Melt the butter in a heavy saucepan over low heat. Stir in the flour to form a thickened paste. Gradually add the milk, increase the flame slightly and bring to a slow boil, stirring constantly as the sauce thickens. If the soup base is too thick, add more milk. For the adult portion you may wish to add a teaspoon of Worcestershire sauce, crushed fresh garlic, ground fresh pepper and salt to taste.

CREAM SOUP VARIATIONS

There is no end to the number of variations for this soup. Use it as a means of persuading your children to eat foods they ordinarily will not touch. Add any of the following to the cream soup base.

Mushrooms. Use a ½ pound of fresh ones. Slice and add directly to the soup base. Browning is unnecessary.

Tomatoes. Use 1 cup, fresh or canned, and purée in a blender before adding to the soup base.

Leftovers. Use 1 cup of meat or vegetables and purée in a blender first.

When adding any of these variations to the soup base simmer for an additional 30 minutes so that all the flavors are well-blended.

SPLIT PEA SOUP

On a cold winter day, nothing hits the spot like a bowl of thick pea soup.

> 1 *package split peas*
> 1 *ham bone left over from a roast*
> 4 *carrots, sliced*
> 4 *stalks celery, sliced*
> 1 *onion, diced*
> 4 *quarts stock or water*

Put all the ingredients into a large pot and bring to a boil over a high flame. When boiling, lower the heat and stir to insure peas do not stick to the bottom of the pot and burn.

Cover and simmer for 2½ hours, stirring occasionally. When done remove the bone and when it has cooled scrape the remaining bits of ham off. Return ham to the soup pot.

Blend enough of baby's portion to freeze some for future use. (See Supplies in the chapter entitled "From Milk to Solids.")

Grind fresh pepper and add a little salt to taste for the older family members. Serve with grated cheese and toasted bread croutons.

BARLEY SOUP

½ *cup barley*
1 *lamb bone left over from a roast*
2 *cups vegetables like celery, carrots, peas and onions*
4 *quarts stock or water*

Put all the ingredients into a large pot and bring to a boil over a high flame. Lower heat and stir barley up from the bottom of the pot so it does not burn. Cover and simmer for 2½ hours, stirring occasionally. When done, remove bone from the pot and allow to cool. Remove any remaining bits of lamb from the bone and return lamb to soup.

Blend baby's portion before adding fresh parsley sprigs, crushed fresh garlic, ground pepper and salt.

If necessary add more water or barley when reheating.

COTTAGE CHEESE AND MEAT CASSEROLE

This makes a wonderful dish for parties as well as for hungry teenagers and small children. Nobody has ever disliked this casserole.

> 1 *package noodles, flat, shell or any others you may like*
> 1 *pound lean round or chuck steak, ground*
> 1 *large can of tomatoes*
> 1 *pound fresh mushrooms, sliced*
> 1 *quart creamed cottage cheese, without salt if possible*

Heat the oven to 350°. Cook the noodles according to package instructions, and drain them thoroughly. You do not have to brown the ground meat first but if you wish to get rid of any excess fat, prepare it while the noodles are boiling. Crumble the meat into a frying pan; do not add any oil. Slowly brown and stir until the meat has released its fat—about five minutes. Drain well.

Combine the noodles and meat with the rest of the ingredients in a large bowl. Add crushed fresh garlic, ground pepper, oregano and basil to the mixture if you think your child is old enough to enjoy their flavors. If not, set aside the child's portion and bake it separately. Add seasoning to the adult's.

Spoon mixture into a well-greased casserole. Bake for one hour. This can be frozen, reheated, served hot or cold.

COTTAGE CHEESE PANCAKES OR WAFFLES

Try this batter for a nourishing breakfast or lunch-time treat.

    4 *eggs, raw*
    ¾ *cup flour (oat or soy combined,*
       buckwheat, whole-wheat, cottonseed
       or unbleached white are acceptable)
    ¾ *teaspoon baking powder*
    ¾ *teaspoon baking soda*
    ¼ *cup whole powdered milk (optional)*
    1 *cup cottage cheese, without salt if pos-*
       sible
    ½ *cup yogurt or sour cream*

Put all the ingredients into a blender or mixing bowl and blend thoroughly. Let the batter stand for 10 minutes. Pour spoonfuls onto a greased hot griddle or waffle iron and cook.

These taste good served with honey, fresh stewed fruit like peaches, pears, blueberries or strawberries. Babies can eat any of them cut up, with their fingers. If you are serving puréed fruit, let the baby try using a spoon. Makes enough pancakes or waffles to feed four.

CHEESE SOUFFLÉ

This recipe was given to us by a dear friend. We have not known it to fail. Our children love it served hot or cold as a leftover.

2 *cups cheddar cheese, grated*
6 *tablespoons unsalted butter*
6 *tablespoons flour, half whole-wheat, half soy or unbleached white*
2 *cups milk, heated slightly*
6 *eggs separated and at room temperature*

Heat the oven to 325°. While the oven is heating grate the cheese if you have not already. In a heavy saucepan, melt the butter slowly over a small flame. Add the flour and stir together to form a paste. Add the heated milk, increase the heat slightly and bring to a slow boil stirring continually. The mixture will thicken.

Lower the flame and add the egg yolk, well-beaten, to the sauce. Gradually add the cheese, stirring as you add. The cheese will melt and thicken the sauce even more.

Beat the egg whites until they are stiff and frothy. Fold the cheese sauce into the egg whites carefully but thoroughly. Pour into a lightly greased, straight-sided casserole or soufflé dish.

Bake for an hour or until set, sometimes a bit more or a bit less time. The top should be medium brown in color. Do not keep opening the oven, particularly during the first 30 minutes. Remove from the oven and serve immediately.

Soufflé goes very nicely with a salad and crusty bread. Leftover it may be served cold for breakfast or lunch the following day.

Notes on making soufflé: We have made this soufflé under many adverse conditions, including mixing the ingredients ahead of time and combining them in different orders. It has never fallen. If your eggs are small, add an extra one. Firm cheeses, such as Colby and Longhorn may be used. A combination gives a good flavor and is an excellent means of using up old cheese. Try using one half whole-wheat and one half soy flour—all soy is too heavy.

If you have small children underfoot, it is easier to grate the cheese, and measure out all the ingredients in advance. We find a heavy aluminum saucepan easier for the thickening process because the cheese and flour do not stick to the bottom. Experts blend the cheese into the egg whites with a wire whisk but an electric beater on low does just as well. And if you want to be fancy, draw a circle around the top of the soufflé just before popping it in the oven, about an inch from the edge of the dish, to give it that funny ridged crust you see in the magazines. It must be served immediately upon removing from the oven and if it cooks much longer than 60 minutes it begins to fall in the oven, so have your guests seated at the table as you carry it to the place of honor. Someone once told me that the secret of this soufflé is the large amount of flour in it; the less flour in a soufflé the harder it is to prepare and the easier it is to fail.

CHEESE BALLS

These can be served alone as a quick lunch or with a salad and vegetables for a nice dinner.

    1 *cup dry pot cheese*

1 *tablespoon unbleached white flour plus
a little extra for rolling*
1 *egg, raw*

Bring one quart of water to a boil in a saucepan. In the meantime, put the dry pot cheese through a coarse sieve, food mill or meat grinder. Add the tablespoon of flour and the egg and mix well. The consistency should be like biscuit dough, smooth and pliable.

Reduce the flame under the water so it just simmers. Form the dough into small balls and roll them lightly in flour. Drop them one by one gently into the water. When the balls float to the surface, they are done. Remove with a slotted spoon and put onto a warm dish. Serve the cheese balls with melted butter, sour cream or yogurt.

If you wish to make this dough into cheese patties, add a bit more flour to the mixture and shape them as you would a flat hamburger. Fry them in butter.

Note: Cottage cheese can be used instead of dry pot cheese but because it contains more liquid you will have to increase the amount of flour and that will change the taste.

SANDY'S SALMON MOUSSE

This is a super meal for a hot day and keeps well for the next day also. It can be made very plain so that small children can eat it—say after 12 months, depending on the baby's ability to handle solids. Or you can spruce it up with a number of optional ingredients—Tabasco® sauce or grated onion for example—if your child is old enough to enjoy them. It really does look best made in a fish mold so if your family really likes this dish, perhaps you can invest in one. Remember to chop the salmon very finely to get rid of the minute bones. You may substitute tuna if you wish.

> 1 *envelope unflavored gelatin*
> ½ *cup mayonnaise, homemade if possible (see recipe in this chapter)*
> ¼ *teaspoon paprika*
> 1 *teaspoon fresh lemon juice*
> 1 *tablespoon fresh grated onion (optional)*
> ½ *teaspoon Tabasco® sauce (optional)*
> 1 *pound can salmon with no additives*
> 1 *tablespoon chopped capers (optional)*
> ½ *cup heavy cream*
> 3 *cups cottage cheese with no salt added if possible*

Dissolve the gelatin in ¼ cup cold water. Add ½ cup boiling water and stir until dissolved. To this add the mayonnaise, paprika and lemon juice. (You may add the onion and Tabasco® sauce here if you are using them.) Chill briefly or until the mixture is the consistency of unbeaten egg whites.

While the gelatin mixture is in the refrigerator, mash the salmon to a fine consistency. If you are using capers, now is the time to add them. Remove the gelatin from the refrigerator and add it to the salmon. Stir well.

With an egg beater or electric mixer whip the

heavy cream until it is stiff. Fold the cream gently but thoroughly into the salmon mixture. Pour it into a 2 quart fish mold or casserole. Add enough cottage cheese to fill the mold, approximately 3 cups. Chill for a good six hours in the refrigerator. Unmold carefully onto a platter and garnish if you wish with lemon slices and watercress.

CAROL'S TEXAS EGG SALAD

This egg salad comes in three varieties to suit any member of the family. It makes a light high-protein lunch for all. The basic mixture serves one adult and two small children or two adults.

>   2 *hardboiled eggs*
>   ½ *cup cottage cheese*

For Babies. Mash the egg yolks with a fork and add to cottage cheese. Serve as is.

For Toddlers. Chop up entire egg and mix with the cottage cheese. Add a little mayonnaise (check the recipe in this chapter for the homemade variety). Serve with lettuce on whole-wheat bread sandwiches cut in quarters.

For Adults. To the toddler variety add:

>   ½ *teaspoon Belgium or French mustard*
>   *Chopped dill, celery, cucumber,*
>   *watercress and onion*
>   *Grated carrot*
>   *Salt and freshly ground pepper to taste*

Serve as a salad or on sandwiches.

GRAN'S NOODLES AND EGGS

This makes a substantial quick supper and is great for those evenings when the babysitter has to prepare a meal for the children. Figure on a half cup cooked noodles and one egg for each small child.

> *Egg Noodles, cooked, ½ cup per child*
> 1 *tablespoon unsalted butter for each ½ cup noodles*
> *Egg, raw, 1 per child*

Boil the noodles according to the directions on the package until they are soft. Drain well. Melt butter in a skillet over a low flame. When it is melted, add in the noodles and stir.

In a bowl, break the egg(s) and beat until well mixed. Pour the egg(s) over the noodles in the skillet. Stir together until thoroughly mixed, and cook until the egg is as soft or dry as you would like.

Accompany this dish with raw vegetable sticks. Zucchini, carrots, celery, cucumbers and red or green pepper go very nicely.

ALY'S EGGS

For this recipe you need a glass double-boiler. We recently invested in one because it does not absorb any of the taste and food particles the way a metal one does. We use it all the time and like to make this recipe for breakfast or a quick supper.

> 1 *tablespoon unsalted butter*

6 *eggs, raw*
1½ *cups milk*

Melt the butter in the top of the double boiler over simmering water. In a bowl beat together the eggs and the milk. Pour the mixture into a double boiler. Cook over a low flame for approximately 20 minutes. The mixture will harden into a custard. If the center is still liquid, loosen the mold from the sides of the pot and continue cooking until hardened.

If your children are older add in a dash of cinnamon, nutmeg, salt and honey when beating together the eggs and milk. Depending on how much honey you add, the custard will be sweeter and more like a dessert. Remember when serving, that eggs retain their heat, so set the dish for baby out to cool.

FLIPPER'S PANCAKES TURNER

This is our adaptation of an old favorite. It is a basic recipe which everyone likes and it needs no sweetener to make it scrumptious. It is super for a Sunday brunch with friends.

1 *cup flour (whole-wheat, soy or a combination)*
½ *cup wheat germ*
½ *cup whole powdered milk (optional)*
2 *teaspoons baking powder*
1 *cup plain yogurt*
¾ *cup milk*
2 *large eggs, raw*
2 *tablespoons unsalted butter or safflower oil*

Sift together flour, wheat germ, powdered milk and baking powder in a large bowl. Add the yogurt, milk, eggs and butter or oil and stir until well blended.

Heat a griddle and grease with butter. Pour on spoonfuls of the batter and flip when little bubbles appear. You can keep pancakes warm in an oven set at a low temperature.

If you wish, add any of the following to the batter: sliced apples or bananas, or for older children and adults, niblets of cooked corn and ground walnuts.

Serve these pancakes with real maple syrup as well as homemade apple sauce or apple butter, ground nuts (exclude for young children), yogurt, sour cream, jellies, brown or maple sugar or a scoop of ice cream (for dessert).

CREPES

A crepe is a thin pancake which is easy to make and used with all kinds of filling variations to make sensational breakfasts, lunches, dinners or desserts.

> 2 *or* 3 *eggs, raw*
> 1¼ *cups water*
> 1½ *cups flour (¾ cup soy, ¾ cup whole-*
>   *wheat or unbleached white)*
> 1 *teaspoon baking powder*

In a mixing bowl, beat together the eggs and water. Gradually add the flour and baking powder and mix thoroughly. This makes a thin batter which will in turn make thin crepes. Let the batter rest for an hour or so if possible.

Heat a crepe pan or heavy skillet with sloping sides, until very hot. Quickly melt a dab of unsalted butter in the pan. Pour enough batter into the pan to just cover the bottom in a thin layer. This will cook quickly so be ready to turn it fast. Cook second side for only a couple of seconds and ease the finished crepe onto a sheet of waxed paper.

Melt a little more butter and repeat the crepe-making process. Have sheets of waxed paper ready to layer between them. Makes about 14–16 five inch crepes. They can be frozen for future use.

Note: Make the smaller children their crepes first: Salt can then be added to the batter for the older family members. Add just a small pinch.

CREPE FILLINGS

Crepes can be filled with almost anything and always taste good. This includes everything from meat sauces and sautéed vegetables to ice cream and stewed fruit. Put a spoonful of filling vertically along the center and fold the right side over and then the left. Serve seam-side down.

Following are a few suggestions for filling your crepes: chopped apples and cinnamon; chopped apples and fried sausage; homemade jelly and whipped cream; fresh strawberries and whipped cream.

For a super elegant dessert stuff the crepe with ice cream and pour homemade chocolate sauce (see the back of your cocoa can for a recipe) over the top.

Sprinkle on crushed fresh mint and nuts. Needless to say this is just an occasional splurge and one not to be eaten by babies.

BLINTZES

Now that you know how to make a basic crepe, you can turn them into terrific blintzes. This recipe came from a friend who adapted it for her sons in order to tempt them into eating more protein. They are very nutritious and make a special brunch treat for adults too. They take time to prepare so it is best to make them the day before and refrigerate for several days in advance and freeze.

> 1 *batch of crepes (see above)*
> 1½ *pounds Farmer cheese (do not substitute cottage cheese, it is not the right consistency)*
> 1 *egg, raw*
> *Raw sugar or honey to taste (the taste should be fairly sweet)*
> *Pinch of cinnamon*

Combine all the ingredients in a mixing bowl. To make a blintz, put a heaping tablespoon (less if the crepe cannot hold so much) in the center of each crepe and fold it like an envelope. Continue until all the crepes and filling have been used.

To serve, slowly melt a dab of unsalted butter in a large skillet and brown blintzes until golden. Top with sour cream, yogurt, applesauce, real maple syrup, canned unsweetened pineapple, homemade jams or apple butter, and serve with sausage or bacon.

DESSERTS

Desserts should not be the heavy and overly sweet meal-enders they tend to be in this country. A piece of fresh fruit or a light pudding is satisfying and certainly better for you than a large piece of cake. Fill up on the more important dishes served at a meal and the need for an empty-calorie, heavy dessert will not be there.

FRUIT SHERBET

This is one of our favorite refreshing desserts enjoyed by both children and adults.

  ½ *tray of ice cubes, cracked*
  1 *cup fruit flavored ice milk*
  ½ *cup fresh berries in season, or peach, pear, banana, peeled and diced*

Combine all the ingredients in a blender and purée. Pour into a freezer bowl and freeze for one hour stirring once after 20 minutes and again 20 minutes later.

YOGURT SHERBET

Another interesting way to make sherbet. This is delicious and cooling on a hot summer day or after a heavy meal.

1   *cup plain yogurt*
1   *cup very ripe fresh fruit,*
    peeled and mashed

The fruit should not be puréed, just mashed slightly so there are still plenty of chunks. Stir fruit into the yogurt. Pour into a freezer bowl and freeze for one hour, stirring once after 20 minutes and again after 20 more.

JUDY'S JAMAICAN GRAPEFRUIT

This is a different type of dessert and for special occasions only. It was created on the island of Jamaica by a friend of Mary's brother.

Fresh grapefruit sections, ½ grapefruit
per person
Condensed milk

Place grapefruit in a bowl and add enough condensed milk to sweeten. When serving, garnish each bowl with a sprig of mint.

HONEY TAPIOCA

This recipe is adapted from the Minute® Tapioca box.

3   *tablespoons tapioca*
3   *tablespoons honey*
2   *cups milk*
1   *egg, raw and separated*
¾   *teaspoon vanilla*

Mix tapioca, 2 tablespoons honey, milk and egg yolk in saucepan. Let stand 5 minutes while you beat the egg white until it becomes foamy.

Cook tapioca until it boils. Turn down heat, stir constantly while it thickens (10 minutes or more). Add 1 tablespoon honey to egg white and beat. Add to tapioca mixture and stir. Add vanilla. Pour into five small dishes and allow to cool.

PEANUT BUTTER DANDIES

These are super delicious. If your children are very young leave out the nuts and make them with smooth rather than crunchy peanut butter. Any or all of the optional ingredients may be added depending, too, on the ages of the children.

> ½ cup honey
> 1½ cups crunchy peanut butter with no additives
> ¼ cup Tigers Milk®
> ¼ cup whole powdered milk (½ cup if you cannot find any Tigers Milk®)
> 1 cup pecans or other unsalted nuts, crushed
> ¼ cup sesame seeds (optional)
> ¼ cup wheat germ (optional)
> ¼ cup coconut, shredded and with no added sugar (optional)
> Carob powder

Mix all the ingredients thoroughly except for the carob powder. Break off pieces and roll into balls the size of walnuts. Roll in carob powder and place on a sheet of waxed paper. Refrigerate for at least an hour and keep any extras refrigerated. This makes about 36.

SUPER-COOKIES

Here is a nutritious, delicious, but quickly prepared old favorite of all children, from the youngest on up.

> 1½ *cups Familia® cereal (or other*
> *Bircher-Benner cereal)*
> ½ *cup dried Tiger's Milk®*
> ½ *cup wheat germ (raw or toasted)*
> ¾ *cup raw sugar, or ½ cup honey*
> ⅓ *teaspoon ground cloves*
> 1 *teaspoon cinnamon*
> ½ *cup melted butter, or oil*
> 2 *eggs, raw*

Heat oven to 350°. Mix all ingredients on the list down to the oil. Add oil and beaten eggs and mix thoroughly. Spoon onto a greased baking sheet.

Bake for 12 to 15 minutes. If you cannot get any of the Swiss cereals substitute oatmeal (dried) and sliced almonds.

SNACKS

Most children need to eat about every three hours, sometimes sooner. It is easy to give your child a cookie every time he or she whines, but it is not healthy. It is just as easy to have on hand various healthy, high protein snacks, devoid of sugars and additives which your child (and you, too, for that matter) do not need.

CRACKERS PLUS

Particularly good in midmorning if lunch will be late (due to an older child's schedule, for example), or after school when older children are exhausted and the little ones need to be stretched for a later dinner hour are unsalted soda crackers with any of the following: a large blob of cottage cheese; thick slices of any good cheese; peanut butter; smear of mashed avocado; homemade jams or apple butter (health food store variety if homemade is out of the question).

RABBIT FOOD

A plate of raw vegetables or fruit to eat plain or with a nice dip makes a good snack or meal appetizer.

Peel if necessary, cut into small pieces and arrange on a platter fresh raw cauliflower, carrots, mushrooms, tomatoes, apples, red and white cabbage, celery, lettuce, red or green peppers, cucumbers, zucchini, avocado, peas in the pod for older children, and shredded raw beets.

In the summer make a dish of melon balls from assorted melons in season and serve plain or sprinkled with unsweetened coconut as a special treat.

NEAT NIBBLES

These are for children who are nongaggers or past the gagging stage.

Sunflower seeds
Unsalted roasted soy beans
Raisins, plain or with unsalted peanuts
Fresh or dried fruits such as apricots, apples, peaches, cut up
Celery stuffed with cream or blue cheese or peanut butter with no additives

OOKERS' GORP

This version of gorp (which is an acronym for "good old raisins and peanuts"—a quick-energy snack used by hikers and bicyclists) was created out of desperation by Ookers' mother when her daughter refused to eat any other traditional baby foods, homemade or commercial. It is different and delicious and we include it to show you what ingenuity can do.

½ cup unsalted peanuts or cashews
½ cup raisins
½ cup ricotta cheese

Mix the nuts and raisins together and put through a food grinder twice. Mix in the ricotta cheese. Voila—Ookers' gorp! (Ookers' real name by the way is Jessica.)

Note: Buy raw nuts in a health food store if possible and roast them yourself.

EGGNOG

This is the everything drink—snack, pick-me-up or nourishing breakfast for babies over one year, tired or in a rush moms and dads.

> 1 *egg, raw*
> 1 *cup milk*
> 1 *teaspoon carob powder or ¼ cup peeled fresh fruit or ½ teaspoon vanilla and 1 teaspoon honey*
> 1 *ice cube, crushed (optional)*

Combine all ingredients in a blender and blend until frothy.

BANANA MILK SHAKE

This makes a terrific snack when your child is really hungry but dinner is not for another couple of hours.

> 1 *cup milk*
> 2 *scoops ice cream (vanilla preferred)*
> 1 *or* 2 *overripe bananas*
> ½ *teaspoon vanilla*

Combine ingredients in a blender. Do not overblend; a minute should be enough time.

SLURPIES

Our son and his friends make these on hot summer days.

> 1 *can frozen orange juice concentrate*
> 1½ *cups water*
> ½ *tray ice cubes, cracked*

Combine all the ingredients in a blender and blend until frothy. Serve immediately in tall glasses with a spoon.

CUBESICLES

These are best eaten when your baby has sufficient manual control to manage them somewhat neatly. However, if you are not worried about a little mess, kids of all ages will enjoy cubesicles.

> ⅓ *cup apple juice*
> ⅓ *cup cranberry juice*
> ⅓ *cup orange juice*
> *or*
> ½ *cup grape juice*
> ½ *cup plain yogurt*
> *or*
> 1 *cup milk*
> 1 *teaspoon carob powder*
> ½ *teaspoon honey*

Combine any of these three recipes in a bowl and pour into an individual cube ice cube tray. Put into freezer. When it is semi-frozen (check after an hour), put ice cream sticks into the center of each one. Freeze for several hours until firm. Cubesicles are great when your child is sick and will not eat anything else you offer.

CHILDREN'S PARTIES

Parties for children, be they birthday, Halloween or spur-of-the-moment, are best when kept to the bare minimum. A few hats, a single small gift for each child, one game in which they can all get involved will suffice.

For younger children we suggest inviting six friends at most for a period of one and a half to two hours, and then include their parents later. Let the children play whatever games they want (within reason), which is possible when you do not have a horde overrunning your house. If you have a yard, plan to have the party outside, weather permitting.

After the children have played for an hour or so serve a meal. Serve the cake and ice cream a little later. We invite the parents to stop in about this time so they can share in the fun of watching the small children's excitement with the cake followed by the opening of the gifts. The adults have cake and coffee while the children play longer.

We have done this several times around supper-time and so have included a dinner dish for our party guests. We wind up with children, parents and several of the neighborhood's favorite babysitters invited for cake and play. The parents sit and talk and by bedtime everyone is relaxed and sleepy. The birthday child is satiated.

SUGGESTED MENU FOR A CHILD'S PARTY

Hamburgers on buns (whole-wheat or English muffins)
Raw vegetable sticks
Pure juice—fresh orangeade or lemonade, grape, apple, but not a part juice, part additive drink
Ice cream
Cake

You might try a good locally made ice cream cake or homemade carrot cake, instead of a traditional flour birthday cake.

Remember, keep it very simple and do not make life hard on yourself. This way everyone, including the parents, will have a good time.

PART IV
THE
APPENDIXES

SUGGESTED READING LIST

Since the first edition of *Making Your Own Baby Food* was published many more articles and books on the subjects of nutrition, world health and hunger, parenting, childbirth and pregnancy have been published.

Each of the following books listed and described are ones we thought you as parents and consumers might find advantageous. They provide a foundation, a basic introduction to the subjects. This is not a complete list and if you are interested you can go on to do further research of your own.

The American Food Scandal, *by William Robbins, New York, William Morrow & Company, 1974.*

An extensive discussion, beautifully written by a *New York Times* reporter, of how large conglomerates have taken over farms and whole sections of states like California. It covers the power politics of behind-the-scenes food decisions like the Russian wheat deal and the dairy lobby. In a chapter entitled "Ambush in the Aisles" the author examines the psychology of shopping. The author spent much time researching and is privy to sources open to few people. Highly informative and often scandalous. Recommended when you have gotten through some of the more basic books on food.

The Chemical Feast, *by James S. Turner, New York, Grossman, 1970.*

An important discussion of how the Food and Drug Administration regulates, or fails to regulate, our food supply. Using specific examples, it examines past frauds and names names. Extensive notes make this an important reference book on the FDA, as well as a primer for those truly interested in food action and the consumer movement.

The Complete Book of Breastfeeding, *by Marvin S. Eiger, M.D. and Sally Wendkos Olds, New York, Workman, 1972.*

Just what its title says it is. A thorough no-nonsense approach to every aspect of nursing your baby and how to handle any problems which may arise. Marvin Eiger is a leading New York pediatrician and Sally Olds is an author and mother who successfully nursed her children and whose confidence and security comes across on every page.

Even if you aren't having any problems with breastfeeding, we recommend it. It contains some of the most beautiful infant photographs we have ever seen. The chapter written specifically for fathers is positive and delightful.

Consumer Beware, *by Beatrice Trum Hunter, New York, Touchstone Book, Simon and Schuster, 1971.*

Thorough coverage of the food industry, additives and supermarkets, with extensive documentation and good end notes for each chapter make this an important book in the struggle to improve the nation's food supply. Part IV, "Sane Alternatives, What's To Be Done?" outlines the problems of the American consumer and the food industry with intelligence and brevity. Some of this book is a rehash of the Margolius book *(The American Food Hoax)* (listed) but it is well done, although probably not as helpful and pragmatic as *The Supermarket Handbook* (listed). Recommended for thoughtful and serious reading on the subject.

The Dictionary of Calories and Carbohydrates, *by Barbara Kraus, New York, Grosset & Dunlap, 1973, and* **The Dictionary of Sodium, Fats, and Cholesterol,** *by Barbara Kraus, New York, Grosset & Dunlap, 1974.*

Both excellent dictionaries of foods listed by brand names, amount, (piece, section, bar), and carbohydrates, sodium, fats, cholesterol and calories contents. Useful for dieters, allergics, new cooks, or as a source book for nutritional information about foods you ordinarily buy and eat.

Food For People Not For Profit, *edited by Catherine Lerza and Michael Jacobson, preface by Ralph Nader, New York, Ballantine, 1975.*

Excellent source book containing reprints of recent articles on nutrition, world food, costs, food production, government and the food industry, with ideas for improvement. A thought-provoking collection of articles for someone already familiar with the food problem rather than the nutritional novice. This book was put together and printed for Food Day, April 17, 1975.

The Great American Food Hoax, *by Sidney Margolius, New York, Dell, 1971.*

"Trying to get through with shopping quickly, instead of treating it as seriously and professionally as earning a living, makes you a target for manipulation. Shopping can be interesting, if not really 'fun', if you treat it as a skill." Developing this skill, working at food shopping, and taking your job as a homemaker seriously are the purpose of this book. Discussions of blown up white "balloon bread" and juice drinks are excellent. Additives such as fat, water, air and sugar are discussed at great length and in specific detail. Charts of cost and nutritional factors for various foods are sprinkled throughout the book which makes this an excellent, although somewhat dated and not always easily understood, sourcebook on food shopping.

The Home Birth Book, *by Charlotte and Fred Ward, Introduction by Ashley Montagu, Ph.D., Washington, D.C., New Perspectives/Inscape Book, 1976.*

A lovely approach to the controversial subject of home birth and one which you might read even if you have had all the babies you ever intend to have. We found it fascinating. The participants included doctors, parents, psychologists and others. Several of our friends have had home births and have attested to its value as an unsurpassable and joyous experience. You owe it to yourself to read this delightful book and share in the experiences of the authors and their friends.

Immaculate Deception *by Suzanne Arms, Boston, Houghton Mifflin, 1975.*

This book describes the problems encountered by pregnant women and some deceptions practiced by obstetricians and others of the medical profession. Whether or not you agree with the thesis, it is important to know that a controversy is raging in medical circles concerning the present practices of childbirth.

Some of the data and statistics will boggle your mind, but from independent research that we have done we conclude her information is accurate and frightening. The stories by mothers about their own childbirth experiences are intriguing; we found the book hard to put down.

Every couple who wants to have a baby, has had a baby or might have a baby owes it to themselves to spend time with this book. It seems to us a landmark on the road to better maternal and infant care.

The New York Times Natural Foods Cookbook, *by Jean Hewitt, New York, Quadrangle Books, 1971.*

A cookbook with a no-nonsense approach to eating wholesome, home-prepared foods. Includes an introduction on the pros and cons of "natural" foods plus chapters on beverages, soups, vegetables, salads, breads. The author takes a sensible, rational approach to food faddism.

The large type with which the book is printed and the placing of only one, or at most two, recipes per page makes this much easier to use than most other cookbooks. The ingredients are listed clearly and separately. The instructions are simple, uncomplicated, exceedingly easy to follow.

The sections on baby foods and candy are well done. This cookbook is recommended as the easiest, most complete basic cookbook for someone who is trying to get their family to eat better. It is a joy to use.

Nutrition Against Disease, *by Dr. Roger Williams, New York, Bantam, 1971.*

Dr. Williams' book may be the most important discussion of nutrition and disease ever written. While not easy to read and crammed full with technical scientific data, it is fascinating. He believes that our cells must be well-fed in order for us to feel well and that "the nutritional microenvironment of our body cells is crucially important to our health and that deficiencies in this environment constitute a major cause of disease." Chapters contain information on obesity, dental disease, heredity and nutrition, alcoholism, old age, food fads, cancer, and more. Since he believes that "Conventional wisdom is never sacred," he is able to examine the relationship between nutrition and disease in a new way. An important book that every person seriously concerned about health should read.

Overweight Causes, Cost and Control, *by Jean Mayer, Consumers Union Edition, Englewood Cliffs, New Jersey, Prentice-Hall, 1969.*

Dr. Mayer examines the psychological factors of obesity. Much of his information is highly technical, but it is worth wading through this excellent reference book since both sides of each issue are presented by this thoughtful, world-renowned nutritionist. Recommended as a book to dip into from time to time but not one to read straight through.

Recipes For Allergics, *by Billie Little, New York, Grosset & Dunlap, 1969.*
This is an excellent primer on what food allergies are and how to control them. The author stresses allergies to corn, wheat, eggs and milk because they are the most prevalent in this country at this time. The recipes appear to be interesting and workable. Notes on specific foods which cause trouble are informative and suggestions for food replacements are included. It seems like a useful book.

The Supermarket Handbook, *by Nikki and David Goldbeck, New York, Harper and Row, 1973.*
This is a cautious, rational approach to the problem of how to obtain better food using the stores in your neighborhood. Included are a section on recycling with specific do's and don'ts and suggestions for simple cleaning agents like soap, water, and elbow grease. Contains simple no-nonsense advice that every cook and house-person should know. Despite the lack of documentation and bibliography, it seems sensible and sound. This book would make an excellent present for someone setting up housekeeping. Many simple nutritious and easy recipes are listed. Specific brands of foods are recommended in each chapter.

Whole Foods For You, *by Lee Fryer and Dick Simmons, New York, Mason & Lipscomb, 1974.*
A highly readable, informative, straightforward

analysis of America's food supply. Concrete suggestions for buying and cooking include recipes and shopping hints. The chapter on the milling process and nutritional value of whole grain breads is excellent. However, the introduction, which is easy to read and packed with information, is not referenced and one should be hesitant to accept everything it says as fact. The lack of a bibliography detracts from the otherwise high quality of this book. Written for the average American housekeeper, it could serve as a basic introduction to the whole subject of food. Contains quotes from experts in the field. It was specifically written to be used by supermarket shoppers, and along with *The New York Times Natural Foods Cookbook* and *The Supermarket Handbook* (both listed) could serve as a practical starting point for the nutritional novice.

Why Your Child Is Hyperactive, *by Ben F. Feingold, M.D. New York, Random House, 1975.*

We feel this book should be read by every parent, teacher, physician, nurse, school administrator—anyone who comes in contact with, and is responsible for children. With the constant labeling of more and more children as "hyperactive" and the dispensing of drugs to combat this condition, it is important to find out some of the causes of this kind of behavior.

Dr. Feingold believes that the additives in our food are causing this behavior, in a kind of allergic reaction. His book offers one aspect of the problem; in fact the allergic reaction to drugs and chemicals may be even greater and more widespread than even he believes.

PROPOSED RULES FOR LABELING BABY FOODS

The Food and Drug Administration (FDA) proposed new rules for labeling infant foods on September 7, 1976. Comments on the rules closed on November 8, 1976 as we were going to press, and undoubtedly a long and tedious set of legal activities will hold up implementation of the rules for the foreseeable future. But, we thought it might be of interest to parents to have a small glimpse of the technicalities that surround food labeling issues. In this appendix appears the complete text of two rules on infant and junior food proposed by the FDA. They are interesting in that the agency was moved to announce the proposals by a public interest group—Center for Science in the Public Interest—which has been waging a steady campaign against debasement of the foods fed to infants, and because the issuance of the regulations and the words used by the FDA in supporting their new rules underline how important the feeding of infants is.

Although this addition is esoteric and not essential to your efforts to feed your infant properly, it does prove that public concern has grown enough to demand government action.

*Text as it appeared in the *Federal Register*, vol. 41, no. 174—September 7, 1976.

DEPARTMENT OF HEALTH, EDUCATION, AND WELFARE

Food and Drug Administration
[21 CFR Part 102]
[Docket No. 76P–0330]
INFANT AND JUNIOR FOODS
Establishment of Common or Usual Name

The Food and Drug Administration is proposing to establish a common or usual name regulation for infant and junior foods, exclusive of infant formulas and milk, which would require a percentage declaration of the characterizing ingredient(s) as part of the common or usual name. Interested persons have until November 8, 1976 to submit comments.

The Commissioner of Food and Drugs received a petition from the Center for Science in the Public Interest, 1779 Church St., NW., Washington, DC 20036, requesting that a common or usual name regulation be established under 21 CFR Part 102 for prepared baby, infant and/or junior foods. The petition requests that such foods be required to bear as part of the name a percentage declaration of the characterizing ingredient(s) and an identification of the age group for which the food is intended, i.e., infant food or junior food. The petition also requests that for infant and junior foods the definition of "characterizing ingredients" (21 CFR 102.1(b)) be expanded to include all ingredients present in amounts equal to or greater than the named ingredients. The petition further requests that §125.5(a) (21 CFR 125.5(a)) be amended to require labeling of all infant foods, including infant formulas, to list in the ingredient statement the percentage of each ingredient present in an amount of 2 percent or more by weight.

This proposal deals with establishing a common or usual name regulation for infant and junior food. Published elsewhere in this issue of the FEDERAL REGISTER is a proposal to amend §125.5(a) to require percentage declaration of ingredients in infant foods. (See FR Doc. 76–26011)

The Commissioner has received correspondence from several persons in support of this petition. Copies of the petition and correspondence in support thereof have been placed on file at the office of the Hearing Clerk, Rm. 4–65, 5600 Fishers Lane, Rockville, MD 20852.

The petitioner states that baby foods, as currently marketed, present a special purchasing problem for the consumer. Because these foods are pureed, strained, and blended it is impossible for consumers to estimate the amounts of important ingredients by the taste or the appearance of the food. The consumer must, therefore, rely upon the label for this information. The petitioner further states that the appearance of baby foods may be misleading when the label fails to reveal the relative amounts of important ingredients. Ingredients emphasized in the product name may appear to be present in amounts greater than is actually the case. The petitioner also asserts that listing ingredients in order of predominance in the ingredient statement provides only a rough guideline as to the actual amounts of the characterizing ingredient(s) in baby food, and that consumers have a right to know the actual amounts of these ingredients in order to make value comparisons between products and to be in a position to evaluate the total impact of these foods on an infant's or child's diet or needs.

The Commissioner agrees that most labels currently used on infant and junior foods do not inform the consumer about the amounts of characterizing ingredient(s). The Commissioner also agrees that the proportion of characterizing ingredient(s) in infant and junior foods, i.e., those ingredients listed in the name of the food or otherwise featured on the label, may have a material bearing on price and consumer acceptance. Section 102.1(b) (21 CFR 102.1(b)) provides that a common or usual name established by regulation may include a declaration of the percentage of any characterizing ingredient(s) when the proportion of such ingredient(s) has a material bearing on price or consumer acceptance.

The Commissioner also agrees that there is a potential for deception because the ingredient(s) listed in the name of infant and junior foods may appear to be present in amounts greater than is actually the case. In view of these facts, the Commissioner is publishing this proposal to require infant and junior foods fabricated from more than one ingredient and prepared in pureed, blended, strained, or bite-size or cereal form, exclusive of milk and infant formulas that simulate human milk or act as complete or partial substitutes for human milk, to declare the percentage of the characterizing ingredient(s) in the food. The Commissioner further proposes that ingredient percentages be based on the weight of the ingredient(s) used to make the food, taking into consideration any losses known to occur because of processing and storage.

The Commissioner proposes that the percentage declaration of characterizing ingredient(s) be in 5-percent increments, expressed as a multiple of 5 and not greater than the actual percentage of the characterizing ingredient(s) in the product. Those characterizing ingredient(s) present in infant and junior foods at levels less than 5 percent would be declared as "less than 5 percent."

Use of 5-percent increments based on a weight/weight declaration of the ingredient(s) in the food will allow for manufacturing variations and analytical limitations. The Commissioner is of the opinion that manufacturers, using reasonable controls and operating in accordance with good manufacturing practices, will be able to label their product accurately using 5-percent increments.

The Commissioner is aware that the accuracy of percentage declaration may not always be determined by analytical means and that analytical evidence, as well as inspectional evidence, will be needed to determine compliance with these regulations.

As explained below, a proposal (proposed amendment of §125.5(a)) to require infant foods to bear, as part of the list of ingredients, a percentage declaration of all ingredients present at levels of 5 percent or more is published elsewhere in this issue of the FEDERAL REGISTER (FR Doc. 76–26011, page 37595). That proposal contains a requirement that ingredients be declared to the nearest multiple of 5 percent. It also notes several possible problems that might occur because of the different requirements in the two proposals for stating the percentage of ingredients that are also characterizing ingredients, and it specifically invites comment on this aspect of the proposals.

The petitioner also requested that the definition of "characterizing ingredient" be expanded to include all ingredients listed in the product name and those ingredients present in amounts equal to or greater than the named ingredients. The petitioner states that to date, only those ingredients that are expensive or named ingredients have been required to be labeled by percentages as part of the common or usual name. The petitioner asserts that without an expanded definition of "characterizing ingredient" the use of fillers, thickening agents, water, and other ingredients may cause consumer deception.

The Commissioner is of the opinion that the term "characterizing ingredient(s)" is adequately defined in §102.1 (b) as any ingredient(s) or component(s) of a food the proportion of which has a material bearing on price or consumer acceptance. An ingredient or component may also be characterizing if the labeling or the appearance of the food may otherwise create an erroneous impression that such ingredient(s) or component(s) is present in amounts greater than is actually the case.

Under the current definition those ingredients listed in the descriptive portion of the name or otherwise featured on the label of infant and junior foods other than in the ingredient statement would be considered characterizing ingredients. Therefore, the proposed regulation would require the common or usual name of infant and junior foods to include a percent declaration of those ingredients listed in the descriptive portion of the name or otherwise featured on the label, except where such ingredients appear only in the ingredient statement or except where expressly permitted or required by other regulations. Such percent declarations are to be listed in the manner and form set forth in §102.1(b).

Fillers, thickening agents, and other ingredients used for their technical or functional effect in food are not necessarily characterizing ingredients even if present in amounts greater than some of the ingredients featured on the label. Some of the named ingredients may be present in small amounts and still be characterizing. The Commissioner is of the opinion that the fact that an ingredient is present in amounts greater than a particular characterizing ingredient is not of itself a sufficiently significant reason to require percentage declaration of these ingredients in the name of a food.

The petitioner stated that "consumers presently base their buying decisions of baby foods on the product name." The Commissioner agrees and therefore must conclude that consumers will base their judgment of product price and acceptability on the amount of those ingredients featured on the label. Once the percentages of the named ingredients are provided, it is apparent what proportion of the food is reserved for noncharacterizing ingredients. The composition of a product bearing the descriptive name "Strained Egg Yolks" and containing egg yolks, water, and salt could be identified either by stating only the amount of egg yolk or by stating, in addition, the amount of water and salt. However, since the consumers' principal concern for purposes of making value comparisons among products is the amount of egg yolk each contains, the Commission believes that their interests are adequately protected by requiring the percentage of that ingredient to be declared.

The petitioner also requested that the common or usual name include an identification of the age group for which the food is intended and cited "infant," "junior" or "toddler" in its examples. The Commissioner points out that some baby foods are promoted for both infants and children from 1 to 4 years of age and that some infant foods can be used well beyond a child's first year, and some junior-type foods can be used earlier than a child's first year. To require a specific term relative to age to be included in the name seems unduly restrictive, and the petitioner does not present any evidence to demonstrate that these terms need to be included in the name of the product.

Elsewhere in this issue of the FEDERAL REGISTER (FR Doc. 76–26011) the Commissioner is proposing to amend §125.5 to require that infant foods bear, as part of the list of ingredients, a percentage declaration of all ingredients present at levels of 5 percent or more. As the Commissioner points out in the preamble to that proposal, a declaration of the percentage of ingredients in infant foods is necessary to enable the consumer to make informed decisions about buying foods used to meet the special dietary needs of the infant. The Commissioner wants to make it clear that the percentage declaration of characterizing ingredients in infant and junior foods that is proposed in this regulation fulfills the separate purpose of facilitating value comparisons among various infant and junior food products by requiring disclosure of the amounts of those ingredients the proportion of which has a material bearing on price or consumer acceptance.

The Commissioner proposes to require that all products initially introduced into interstate commerce on or after January 1, 1978, comply with the final regulation promulgated on the basis of this proposal.

The Commissioner has carefully considered the environmental effects of the proposed regulation and, because the proposed action will not significantly affect the quality of the human environment, has concluded that an environmental impact statement is not required. The Commissioner has also carefully considered the inflation impact of the proposed regulation as required by Executive Order 11821, OMB Circular A–107, and the Guidelines issued by the Department of Health, Education, and Welfare, and no major inflation impact has been found. Copies of the FDA environmental and inflation impact assessments are on file with the Hearing Clerk, Food and Drug Administration.

Therefore, under the Federal Food, Drug, and Cosmetic Act (secs. 201(n), 403(a), 701(a), 52 Stat. 1041 as amended, 1047–1048 as amended, 1055 (21 U.S.C. 321(n), 343(a), 371(a))) and under authority delegated to the Commissioner (21 CFR §5.1) recodification published in the FEDERAL REGISTER of June 15, 1976 (41 FR 24262)), it is proposed that Part 102 be amended in Sub-part B by adding new §102.26 to read as follows:

§102.26 Prepared infant or junior foods.

The common or usual name of a food represented as infant food (exclusive of milk and infant formulas that simulate human milk or act as complete or partial substitutes for human milk) for persons not more than 12 months of age, or junior food, for children from 1 to 4 years of age, and prepared from more than one ingredient shall include:

(a) A descriptive term meeting the requirements of §102.1(e).

(b) A statement of the percentage of all ingredients listed in the descriptive portion of the name, or otherwise featured on the label, except where such ingredients appear only in the ingredient statement or except where expressly permitted or required by other regulations. Such percent declarations are to be listed in the manner and form set forth in §102.1(b). The percentage of each such ingredient, which shall be identified by its common or usual name, shall be declared in 5-percent increments, expressed as a multiple of 5 and not greater than the actual percentage of the ingredient in the product, except that the percentage of any ingredient present at less than 5 percent may be declared as "less than 5 percent." Dehydrated forms of ingredients shall be calculated on the basis of the hydrated weight.

Interested persons may, on or before November 8, 1976, submit to the Hearing Clerk, Food and Drug Administration, Rm. 4–65, 5600 Fishers Lane,

Rockville, MD 20852, written comments (preferably in quintuplicate and identified with the Hearing Clerk docket number found in brackets in the heading of this document) regarding this proposal. Received comments may be seen in the above office during working hours, Monday through Friday.

Dated: August 30, 1976.

JOSEPH P. HILE,
Acting Associate, Commissioner for Compliance.

[FR Doc. 76–26010 Filed 9–3–76; 8:45 am]

[21 CFR Part 125]
[Docket No. 76P–0329]
INFANT FOODS
Percentage Declaration of Ingredients

The Food and Drug Administration (FDA) is proposing to require that infant food labels bear percentage declaration of ingredients when such ingredients are present at levels of 5 percent or more in making the finished food. Interested persons have until November 8, 1976 to submit comments.

The Food and Drug Administration has received a petition from the Center for Science in the Public Interest, 1779 Church St., NW., Washington, DC 20036. The petition requests that §125.5(a) (21 CFR 125.5(a)) be amended to require the label of all infant foods to list the percentage of each ingredient that is present in an amount of 2 percent or more by weight. The petition also requested that a common or usual name regulation be established for baby food under 21 CFR Part 102. Published elsewhere in this issue of the FEDERAL REGISTER is a proposal for establishing a common or usual name regulation for infant and junior foods. (See FR Doc. 76–26010.)

The Commissioner of Food and Drugs has received correspondence from several individuals in support of this petition. Copies of the petition and correspondence in support thereof have been placed on file at the office of the Hearing Clerk, Rm. 4–65, 5600 Fishers Lane, Rockville, MD 20852.

The petitioner proposes to amend §125.5(a) to read as follows:

If a food (other than a dietary supplement of vitamins and/or minerals alone) purports to be or is represented for special dietary use for infants, the label shall bear, if such food is fabricated from two or more ingredients, the common or usual name of each ingredient including spices, flavorings and coloring and the percentage of each ingredient present in an amount of 2 percent or more by weight.

As grounds in support of this request the petitioner states that FDA has explicitly defined baby foods as "special dietary foods" and that because of the unique role baby foods play in the development of a child, these foods should be labeled with the percentages of all major ingredients. The petitioner states that because commercial baby foods are frequently the only nourishment that infants receive, aside from milk or formula, parents should be able to compare brands and select the brands that have the proportion of ingredients they want their child to receive. If parents want to limit a child's intake of meat, sugar, starch, or salt, the petitioner asserts that there should be adequate information on the label to permit them to do so effectively.

The petitioner also states that the use of fillers, thickening agents, and water dilutes the nutrient content of these foods; as a result, commercially prepared baby foods have a lower nutrient density than home-prepared foods. The semi-solid appearance of some of these foods, however, leads consumers to assume that these foods have a nutritional density similar to those of home-prepared recipes.

The Commissioner agrees that foods purporting to be or represented as food for infants, i.e., persons under 12 months of age, are foods for special dietary use and subject to the requirements of §125.5. The Commissioner points out, however, that the petition uses the term "baby food" as being synonymous with infant, junior or toddler food. Currently, foods represented solely for use as junior or toddler food, i.e., for persons from 1 to 4 years of age, are not considered as foods for special dietary use. The history of the proceedings leading to the establishment of §125.5 demonstrates clearly that infants possess a number of unique physical and physiological characteristics that affect their feeding requirements and set them apart from older children. The Commissioner realizes that many of these foods can be and are being used for both infants and children over 12 months of age. If such foods are represented for use by both groups, they are considered to be foods for special dietary use. The manufacturer, however, does have the option of representing the food only for use by children over 12 months of age. The petition does not make it clear whether the requested amendment to §125.5 would include those foods represented solely for use as junior or toddler food.

In discussing grounds in support of the requested amendment, the petition also distinguishes infant, junior and toddler food from infant formula, yet §125.5 does include infant formulas. It is not clear from the petition whether the requested amendment to §125.5 would include infant formulas.

The Commissioner is of the opinion that for the purposes of this proposal only infant foods other than infant formulas should be considered. Infant foods have clearly been identified as foods for special dietary use and as such require additional label information. Infant formulas are already required by §125.5(c) to bear additional label information concerning composition. Foods represented solely as junior or toddler food, i.e., for persons from 1 to 4 years of age, are not considered foods for special dietary use under §125.5.

As the petition points out, commercially prepared infant foods containing added water may have a lower nutrient density than corresponding foods prepared in accordance with home recipes. The Commissioner points out, however, that most home recipes are not designed specifically for infants and that the addition of water and thickening agents to commercial products may have very valid functional purposes. The addition of water does not mean that commercially prepared infant foods are inadequate to meet a child's nutritional needs. The petition, furthermore, does not suggest such a conclusion. The Commissioner does agree, however, that because these foods are pureed, strained, and blended and thickened to give a semisolid consistency, there is a potential for consumers to conclude that these foods have nutrient densities similar to those prepared at home, which they may or may not possess. In the absence of percentage declaration of ingredients, it is impossible to compare commercial infant foods with those prepared in the home.

The Commissioner realizes that parents have a responsibility to exercise control over the nutritional quality of a child's diet and to safeguard a child's future health and welfare. It is obvious that a consumer's perception of the nutritional value of infant foods will affect the nutritional quality of a child's diet.

The Commissioner is also aware that some consumers attribute a dietary significance to the proportion of certain ingredients contained in infant foods. Many current theories or hypotheses concerning the diets of young children and the effects of diets on the future health of children are being accepted by consumers as facts. For example, the relationship between infant overfeeding and adult obesity and heart disease are theories currently being discussed by clinical nutritionists and other medical specialists. Consumers, however, are being led to believe that this theory is a well established fact even though there is no conclusive evidence to show that overfeeding in infancy results in adult obesity or leads to the development of adult heart disease. In addition, parents are being cautioned against baby foods containing added starch or sugar because it is alleged that the presence of these ingredients in baby food results in, among other things, infant overfeeding. However, there is no evidence that the presence of starch or sugar in baby foods contributes per se to infant overfeeding.

This type of social response to medical discussion is not unusual or unique to infant foods. The Commissioner points out that the action proposed here is not intended to lend credence to any of the current theories or hypotheses that are currently being discussed with regard to baby foods.

It is apparent that, for a variety of reasons, a substantial number of consumers consider the proportion of ingredients in infant food to be important to the dietary welfare of their children. The Commissioner is of the opinion that parents have the right to be informed concerning the proportion of ingredients in infant foods so that they, acting alone or with the advice of a physician, may judge the usefulness of a particular food in the overall dietary regime they have selected for their children and so that they may compare commercial infant foods with one another and with those foods prepared in the home.

Section 403(j) of the Federal Food, Drug, and Cosmetic Act authorizes the Commissioner to establish regulations that prescribe necessary label information required to appear on foods for special dietary use in order to fully inform purchasers as to their value for such uses.

The Commissioner is, therefore, proposing that §125.5 be amended to require all infant foods, except milk and infant formulas that simulate human milk or act as complete or partial substitutes for human milk, to list the percentage of those ingredients present at 5 percent or more in the finished food. This proposal does not include infant formulas because they are already required by §125.5(c) to be labeled with detailed information concerning composition.

In addition, the Commissioner is proposing that ingredient percentages be expressed in 5 percent increments to the nearest multiple of 5 based upon the weight of ingredients used in making the finished food.

The Commissioner realizes that in proposing a regulation for a percentage declaration of ingredients for infant foods a number of fundamental questions are raised that must be answered before an optimum system for declaring percentages of ingredients can be established.

Key questions relative to infant foods (exclusive of infant formulas) and to other "baby" foods that may serve as foods for both infants and toddlers are enumerated below. The Commissioner urges that respondents address those questions relevant to their interests and knowledge of infant and related foods, in addition to providing any other comments concerning these foods they deem appropriate. The Commissioner also urges that viable alternative solutions be presented for consideration, if such alternatives exist. The questions are as follows:

1. The proposal specifies that percentage declarations be made on the basis of the weight of the ingredients used to make the finished food, i.e., quantitative "recipe" labeling. Are there alternative methods of calculating

percentages of ingredients that would be more informative to consumers? How can ingredient percentages be calculated to take into consideration the loss or transformation of certain ingredients during the processing and storage of infant foods? Water is an example of an ingredient that may be lost in part during processing. Starch is an example of an ingredient that may be transformed into dextrins or other lower molecular weight carbohydrates during the processing of storage of infant foods.

2. The proposal specifies that percentage declarations be made for each ingredient present at a level of 5 percent or more by weight. The 5-percent level is proposed on the basis of analytical limitations and from a limited knowledge of manufacturing variations. Is there an alternative higher or lower threshold that has a sound basis and would provide consumers with sufficient ingredient information to fully inform them as to the value of these foods for special dietary use? What additional information could be obtained by requiring a different threshold?

3. The proposal specifies that percentage declarations be made in 5 percent increments to the nearest multiple of 5, based upon the input weight of the ingredient. Is there an alternative increment spacing that will allow for manufacturing variation without leading to distortions of ingredient information? As explained below, a proposal to establish a common or usual name for infant and junior foods is being published elsewhere in this issue of the FEDERAL REGISTER (FR Doc. 76–26010). That proposed regulation contains a requirement that characterizing ingredients be declared in 5 percent increments to a multiple of 5, not to exceed the amount actually present. This may lead to differences between the percentages of characterizing ingredients declared as part of the common or usual name and the percentage of characterizing ingredients declared as part of the list of ingredients in the ingredient statement.

Would such differences result in consumer confusion or deception? What would be the result of requiring a percentage of a particular ingredient to be identical in the percentage declaration of characterizing ingredients and the list of ingredients? If both percentages are not permitted to exceed the actual percentage, as provided in the common or usual name proposal, would this result in an unacceptably inaccurate percentage statement in the list of ingredients as compared with permitting the declaration to be rounded to the nearest multiple of 5 percent? If both percentages are required to be stated to the nearest multiple of 5 percent, as provided in this proposal, would this result in an unacceptable overstatement of the amount of characterizing ingredient declared as part of the common or usual name? What other approaches might be considered?

4. It is evident that there must be cost/benefit considerations given to the requirements of this proposal. The Commissioner, therefore, urges consumers to respond specifically to the following questions. What additional benefits are made possible by the requirements of this proposal that are not available under the current labeling requirements for infant foods that include the listing of ingredients in descending order of predominance? How much are consumers willing to pay in terms of increased food prices for these benefits? Would consumers be willing to pay 1 percent more for percentage declaration of ingredients on infant food labels? Five percent more? Similarly, the Commissioner urges manufacturers to respond specifically as to what cost increases could be expected as a result of the requirements of this proposal. What increases in production, labeling, and marketing costs will result from promulgation of the proposed regulation?

5. The proposal would require percent declaration of ingredients put into the food at the point of formulation if the amounts are equal to or greater than 5 percent. Recognizing that carbohydrates, proteins and fats, particularly car-

bohydrates, might be supplied by more than one ingredient, would it be insufficiently informative and misleading to declare only the added sugar, for example, and not also indicate the amount or proportion of total sugars present as a result of the combination of several ingredients?

For example, specific added ingredients such as sucrose may also be present in other ingredients used in the formulation of the food. Will consumers interpret a percentage declaration for sucrose to mean the total amount of sucrose present in the food or only the amount of sucrose added specifically as sucrose? What other potentially misleading circumstances may arise when infant foods declare ingredients by percentages?

The Commissioner again urges all interested parties to respond to this proposal. In order to establish a sound basis for the establishment of a percentage declaration requirement, the Commissioner is seeking as large a body of scientific information and reasoned public opinon as possible on this matter, which on the surface may appear relatively simple but which is in fact quite complex.

Elsewhere in this issue of the FEDERAL REGISTER (FR Doc. 76–26010) the Commissioner is proposing to amend Part 102 to require that infant and junior foods bear as part of the common or usual name percentage declaration of any characterizing ingredients.

As the Commissioner points out in the preamble to the common or usual name proposal, a declaration of the percentage of any characterizing ingredients is necessary for both infant and junior foods to facilitate value comparisons and to provide positive disclosure of those ingredients the proportion of which has a material bearing on price or consumer acceptance. The Commissioner points out, however, that a requirement for the disclosure of ingredient percentages for infant foods fulfills a separate labeling purpose.

Infant foods have been identified as foods for special dietary use and as such the utility of these foods depends upon whether they meet physiological needs peculiar to infants. Those needs are independent of the proportion of any characterizing ingredients that may be present.

At the same time, infant and junior foods are still foods of the marketplace and consumers need to be informed as to the percentages of ingredients that have a material bearing on price or consumer acceptance, i.e., characterizing ingredients, in order to be able to make value comparisons between competing products.

The Commissioner proposes to require that all products initially introduced into interstate commerce on or after January 1, 1978, comply with the final regulation promulgated on the basis of this proposal.

The Commissioner has carefully considered the environmental effects of the proposed regulation and, because the proposed action will not significantly affect the quality of the human environment, has concluded that an environmental impact statement is not required. The Commissioner has also carefully considered the inflation impact of the proposed regulation as required by Executive Order 11821, OMB Circular A–107, and the Guidelines issued by the Department of Health, Education, and Welfare, and no major inflation impact has been found. Copies of the FDA environmental and inflation impact assessments are on file with the Hearing Clerk, Food and Drug Administration.

Therefore, under the Federal Food, Drug, and Cosmetic Act (secs. 201(n), 403(j), 701(e), 52 Stat. 1041, 1048, and 1056 as amended by 70 Stat. 919 and 72 Stat. 948 (21 U.S.C. 321(n), 343(j), 371(e))) and under authority delegated to the Commissioner (21 CFR 5.1) (recodification published in the FEDERAL REGISTER of June 15, 1976 (41 FR 24262)) it is proposed that Part 125 be amended by revising paragraph (a) of §125.5 to read as follows:

§125.5 Label statements relating to infant food.

(a) If a food (other than a dietary supplement of vitamins and/or minerals alone) purports to be or is represented for special dietary use for infants and is fabricated from two or more ingredients, the label shall bear:

(1) The common or usual name of each ingredient including spices, flavoring, and coloring.

(2) A percentage declaration for each ingredient in the food at a level of 5 percent or more by weight. The percentage of each such ingredient shall be based on the weight of the ingredient used to make the finished food and shall be declared in 5 percent increments to the nearest multiple of 5 based on the weight of the ingredient(s). Percentage declarations shall be in parentheses following the name of the ingredient(s), except that milk and infant formulas that simulate human milk or act as complete or partial substitutes for human milk, as specifically covered under paragraph (c) of this section, are exempt from the requirements of ths paragraph.

* * * * *

Interested persons may, on or before November 8, 1976, submit to the Hearing Clerk, Food and Drug Administration, Rm. 4–65, 5600 Fishers Lane, Rockville, MD 20852, written comments (preferably in quintuplicate and identified with the Hearing Clerk docket number found in brackets in the heading of this document) regarding this proposal. Received comments may be seen in the above office during working hours, Monday through Friday.

Dated: August 30, 1976.

JOSEPH P. HILE,
Acting Associate, Commissioner for Compliance.

[FR Doc. 76–26011 Filed 9–3–76; 8:45 am]

NOTES

PART I   GETTING IN GEAR

CHAPTER 1: A GENERAL OVERVIEW

1. Thomas Y. Canby, "Can The World Feed Its People?," *National Geographic,* July, 1975, p. 22.

2. Ibid.

3. Ibid.

4. Ibid.

5. Ibid, p. 23.

6. In addition to the article cited above, which provides an excellent overview of the problem of world hunger, you might also want to look into the question of bottlefeeding of babies in underdeveloped countries. For more information contact Leah Margulies at the Interfaith Center on Corporate Responsibility, 475 Riverside Drive, Room 566, New York, N.Y. 10027, (212) 870-2294.

CHAPTER 2: THREE BASIC PRINCIPLES

1. "Review of Studies of Vitamin and Mineral Nutrition in the United States (1950–1968)," *Journal of Nutrition Education,* vol. 1, no. 2. supp. 1, Fall 1969, p. 54.

2. *Final Report,* White House Conference on Food, Nutrition and Health, December, 1969, p. 38.

3. The quotations in this paragraph are from *Summaries of Reports,* summaries of the 25 forums meeting at the White House Conference on Children in Washington, D.C., 1970, and released by the Conference: pp. 15–16.

4. Russell J. Bunai, Jr., "A Pediatrician's Point of View," *The Home Birth Book,* Charlotte and Fred Ward (Washington, D.C., New Perspectives/ Inscape, 1976), p. 53.

5. Ben F. Feingold, M.D., *Why Your Child is Hyperactive* (New York: Random House, 1975), p. 96.

CHAPTER 3: THE PRENATAL DIET

1. Margaret A. Ribble, *The Rights of Infants,* (New York: Columbia University Press, 1962), p. 9.

2. Margaret Markham, "Even Before You Know the Baby Is There," *Family Health,* June, 1971, p. 45. This is a special issue on good nutrition and health. This article traces in great detail the development of the embryo during the first two months after conception and describes the nutritional requirements needed at each stage of development. *Family Health* also recommends the book *From Conception to Birth* by Drs. Robert Rugh and Landrum Shettles.

3. Benjamin Spock, M.D. and Miriam E. Lowenberg, Ph.D., *Feeding Your Baby and Child* (Boston: Little Brown and Company, 1955).

PART II
WHAT YOU SHOULD KNOW ABOUT THE BABY FOOD INDUSTRY

CHAPTER 1: NUTRITIONAL IGNORANCE

1. Roger J. Williams, *Nutrition Against Disease* (New York: Pitman Publishing Corp., 1971), p. 198.

2. Ross Hume-Hall, *Food for Nought,* new ed. (New York: Harper & Row Medical, 1974), p. 211.

3. *World Health Organization Technical Report #228,* 1962, p. 6.

4. "What Population Explosion?," *Forbes,* March 1, 1967, p. 60.

5. *Printers' Ink,* July 23, 1965, p. 61.

6. "How to Feed Profits As Well As Babies," *Business Week,* January 8, 1966, pp. 64–66.

7. "Infant Feeding Practices 1966: Salt Content of the Modern Diet," *American Journal of Diseases of Children,* 111, (1966), p. 372.

8. "The Lower Birthrate Crimps the Baby-Food Market," *Business Week,* July 13, 1974, p. 44.

9. G. J. Fruthaler, M.D., "Can Allergy Be Prevented?," *Southern Medical Journal,* vol. 58 (1965), p. 836.

10. A. M. Butler and I. J. Wolman, "Trends in the Early Feeding of Supplementary Foods to Infants," *Quarterly Review of Pediatrics,* vol. 9 (1954): p. 63.

11. "How Consumers Buy Baby Needs," *Supermarketing,* September, 1969, p. 55.

CHAPTER 2: A THREATENED INDUSTRY

1. Weekly Report, Community Nutrition Institute, Washington, D.C., February, 12, 1976, p. 8.

2. Jean Mayer, Making Baby's Food At Home, *Washington Post,* February 26, 1976, p. D 17.

3. These quotes are included in a letter from Dr. Samuel J. Fomon, Professor, University of Iowa Hospitals and Clinics, University of Iowa, Iowa City, Iowa to Robert B. Wieloszynski, Department of Law, 420 City Hall, Syracuse. N.Y.

4. Frederick North, Jr., M.D., *News and Comments,* American Academy of Pediatrics, February, 1976, p. 11.

5. Ibid.

6. "Are Baby Foods Good Enough For Babies?," *Consumers Report,* September, 1975, p. 528–532.

7. Ibid., p. 532.

8. Ibid.

9. Phyllis Battelle, "Assignment America—A Notion That Jarred the Nation," King Features Syndicate, February 25, 1976.

10. Weekly Report, p. 8.

CHAPTER 3: YOU DON'T ALWAYS GET WHAT YOU NEED

1. James Turner interview with Dr. I. J. Hutchings taped for "The Nader Report," WGBH-TV, Boston, at Gerber Baby Food headquarters, Fremont, Mich., August 3, 1970.

2. D. B. Jelliffe, "Commerciogenic Malnutrition? Time for a Dialogue," *Food Technology,* February, 1971, p. 56.

3. R. Burt Gookin before the Select (McGovern) Committee on Nutrition and Human Needs of the United States Senate, Part 13C, Nutrition and Private Industry, July 28, 1969, p. 4563.

4. Personal Communication, Dr. John Olney to James Turner, March, 1970.

5. Ralph Nader, "Baby Foods: Can You (and Your Baby) Afford Them?," *McCall's,* November, 1970, p. 36.

6. T. W. Redding and A. V. Schally, "Effects of Monosodium Glutamate on the Endocrine Axis in Rats." Paper delivered at Federation of American Societies for Experimental Biology, Atlantic City, N.J. meeting, April 14, 1970.

7. Enclosure with letter sent by Dan Gerber to American doctors on October 23, 1970, in response to the Nader article, "Baby Foods," *McCall's.*

8. Personal Communication from Dr. Robert

Stewart to Liane Reif-Lehrer, Department of Ophthalmology, Harvard Medical School.

9. Dr. John Olney, Ho, Oi Lan, M.D. and Rhee, Vesela, M.D., *New England Journal of Medicine,* August 23, 1973, p. 391–395.

10. Letter to editor from Liane Reif-Lehrer, *New England Journal of Medicine,* December 4, 1975, p. 1204.

11. *Safety and Suitability of Salt for Use in Baby Foods,* Subcommittee on Safety and Suitability of MSG and Other Substances in Baby Foods, Food Protection Committee, Food Nutrition Board, National Research Council, National Academy of Sciences, September, 1970.

12. Ibid., p. 11.

13. Ibid., p. 12.

14. *Handbook on Recommended Dietary Allowances,* National Academy of Sciences, 8th ed., 1974, p. 89.

15. "Should You Make/Buy Your Baby Food," *Mothers' Manual,* January–February, 1976, p. 10.

16. Ibid.

17. Recommended Dietary Allowances, p. 89.

18. Ibid., p. 90.

19. Ibid., p. 89.

20. *Safety and Suitability of Salt,* p. 12.

21. *Safety and Suitability of Modified Starches for Use in Baby Foods,* Subcommittee on Food Protection, Committee on Food and Nutrition, National

Research Council, National Academy of Sciences, September, 1970, p. 3.

22. Ibid., p. 1.

23. Memorandum on modified starches prepared by Kenneth Schlossberg, staff counsel to the Select (McGovern) Committee, July, 1969. In files of the Committee.

24. "Should You Make/Buy Your Baby Food," p. 10.

25. Ibid., p. 14.

26. *Safety and Suitability of Modified Starches,* pp. 2, 23.

27. Gerber letter to doctors.

28. *Research Explores Nutrition and Dental Health,* Department of Health, Education and Welfare, Public Health Service, National Institute of Health, 1970, p. 5.

29. Gerber letter to doctors.

30. Jean Mayer, Memorandum to Select (McGovern) Committee, July, 1969.

PART III   THE ALTERNATIVES
CHAPTER 1: BREASTFEEDING

1. "Dr. David Reuben Answers Yours Questions About Breast-Feeding," *McCall's,* May, 1971, p. 64.

2. Margaret A. Ribble, *The Rights of Infants* (New York: Columbia University Press, 1962), p. 105.

3. Betty J. Oseid, "Breast-Feeding and Infant Health," *Clinical Obstetrics and Gynecology,* vol. 18, no. 2, p. 149–173.

4. Dr. Oseid is quoting from American Academy of Pediatrics: Standards and Recommendations for Hospital Care of Newborn Infants, 5th ed. (Evanston, Ill.: AAP, 1971).

5. Oseid, "Breast-Feeding," p. 170.

6. D. B. Jelliffe, "Unique Properties of Human Milk," *Journal of Reproductive Medicine,* vol. 14, no. 4, p. 136.

7. Ibid., p. 135.

8. Ibid.

9. Oseid, "Clinical Obstetrics," p. 158.

10. Ted Greiner, *The Promotion of Bottle Feeding by Multinational Corporations: How Advertising and the Health Professions Have Contributed,* Cornell International Nutrition Monograph Series, no. 2 (1975), p. iii. Copies may be obtained by writing to Dr. Michael Latham, Division of Nutritional Sciences, Savage Hall, Cornell University, Ithaca, N.Y. 14853.

11. Ibid., p. iv.

12. Jelliffe, "Unique Properties," p. 136.

CHAPTER 2: FROM MILK TO SOLIDS

1. Helen A. Guthrie, M.S., "Effects of Early Feeding of Solid Food on Nutritive Intake of Infants," *Pediatrics,* vol. 38, no. 5, November, 1966, p. 879.

2. Ibid.

Companies specializing in wholesome food products include:

Plus Products. Examine their catalog for vitamins, Tiger's Milk®, yogurt cultures and more. You can find them in many health food stores.

Walnut Acres. A farm specializing in nonchemically fertilized products. Listed in their catalog are many homemade items such as apple butter, peanut butter, pickles, canned fruits in natural juices, brown rice, cereals, grains and flours of all kinds. They are located in Penn's Creek, Pennsylvania 17862.

Organizations working on nutrition include:
International Academy of Metabology
1000 E. Walnut Street
Pasadena, California 91106

International College of Applied Nutrition
Box 386
La Habra, California 90631

Society of Clinical Ecology (for allergy information)
109 W. Olive Street
Fort Collins, Colorado 80521

BOOK & PAMPHLET BIBLIOGRAPHY

Cardozo, Peter, and Menten, Ted. *The Whole Kids Catalog,* New York, Bantam, 1975.

Carper, Jean. *The Brand Name Nutrition Counter,* New York, Bantam, 1975.

Davis, Adelle. *Let's Cook It Right,* new rev. ed., New York, Harcourt, Brace & World, 1962.

Davis, Adelle. *Let's Have Healthy Children,* rev. ed., New York, Harcourt, Brace & World, 1959.

Eiger, Martin S., M.D., and Olds, Sally Wendkos. *The Complete Book of Breastfeeding,* New York, Workman, 1972.

Facts About Breast Feeding, Evansville, Indiana, Mead Johnson, 1968.

Feingold, Ben F., M.D. *Why Your Child Is Hyperactive,* New York, Random House, 1975.

Foods for Baby, Fremont, Michigan, Gerber, 1963.

Fitzgerald, Dorothy; Herman, Ester; Ventre, Fran; and Long, Tina. *Home Oriented Maternity Experience,* Washington, D.C., H.O.M.E., Inc., 1976.

Happy Mealtimes for Your Baby, New York, Beech-Nut, 1968.

Hatfield, Antoinette Kuzmanich; and Stanton, Peggy Smeeton. *Help! My Child Won't Eat Right,* Washington, D.C., Acropolis, 1973.

Hume-Hall, Ross. *Food For Nought: The Decline in Nutrition,* New York, Harper & Row, 1974.

Hunter, Beatrice Trum. *The Natural Foods Cookbook,* New York, Simon and Schuster, 1961.

Jelliffe, D. B. "Nutrition in Early Childhood, Part I: Nutrition and Health," *World Review of Nutrition and Dietetics* 19, edited by G. H. Bourne, Phiebig, 1974.

Kelly, Marguerite, and Parsons, Elia. *The Mother's Almanac,* Garden City, New York, Doubleday, 1975.

Lappe, Frances Moore. *Diet For A Small Planet,* New York, Friends of the Earth/Ballantine, 1971.

Larson, Gena. *Better Food for Better Babies,* New Canaan, Connecticut, Keats, 1972.

Lerza, Catherine, and Jacobson, Michael, eds. *Food For People Not For Profit,* New York, Ballantine, 1975.

Maternal Nutrition and the Course of Pregnancy, Washington, D.C., National Academy of Sciences, 1970.

New York City's Baby Book, New York, Department of Health, 1955.

Osterizer Guide for Feeding Baby Better, Milwaukee, Wisconsin, John Oster Manufacturing, 1967.

"Review of Studies of Vitamin and Mineral Nutrition in the United States (1950–1968)," *Journal of Nutrition Education,* Fall, 1969.

Robbins, William. *The American Food Scandal,* New York, William Morrow, 1974.

Ribble, Margaret, M.D. *The Rights of Infants: Early Psychological Needs and Their Satisfaction,* New York, Columbia University Press, 1962.

Should Milk Drinking By Children Be Discouraged?, Committee on Nutrition, American Academy of Pediatrics, April, 1974.

Spock, Benjamin, M.D. and Lowenberg, Miriam E., Ph.D. *Feeding Your Baby and Child,* New York, Duell, Sloan and Pearce, 1955.

Ward, Charlotte and Fred. *The Home Birth Book,* Washington, D.C., New Perspectives/Inscape Book, 1976.

White House Conference on Food, Nutrition and Health, Final Report, Washington, D.C., U.S. Government Printing Office, 1970.

Williams, Roger J. *Nutrition Against Disease,* New York, Pitman Publishing Company, 1971.

White Paper On Infant Feeding Practices, Washington, D.C., Citizens' Committee on Infant Nutrition, Center for Science in the Public Interest, 1974.

MAGAZINE BIBLIOGRAPHY

Bell, Joseph N. "When Babies Go Hungry," *Good Housekeeping,* June 1974.

"Breast or Bottle," *Science,* May 31, 1974.

Canby, Thomas Y. "Can the World Feed Its People," *National Geographic,* July, 1975.

Feingold, Ben F. "Hyperkinesis and Learning Disabilities Linked to Artificial Food Flavors and Colors," *American Journal of Nursing,* May, 1975.

"First Report of the Preliminary Findings and Recommendations of the Interagency Collaborative Group on Hyperkinesis," submitted to the Assistant Secretary for Health, United States Department of Health, Education and Welfare.

"Food—How Do You Feel About Food? What Do You Know About Food?," *Redbook,* May 1974. This article contains the results of a *Redbook* reader survey conducted by the magazine's editorial and research departments.

"Foreword," *World Review of Nutrition and Dietetics* 16 (1973).

"Formula for Malnutrition," Corporate Information Center Brief, Consumers Union of the United States, Inc., 1975.

Grace, Princess of Monaco, "Why Mothers Should Breastfeed Their Babies," and "Some Other Glamorous Women Tell Why They Believe in Breastfeeding," *Ladies' Home Journal*, August, 1971.

Hunter, Beatrice Trum. "Nitrite Additives in Meat Products: A Hazard for Consumers of Bacon, Frankfurters, Corned Beef, Luncheon Meats, and Other Cured Food Products," *Consumers' Research Magazine*, May, 1975.

"Infant Mortality—Progress and Problems," *Population Bulletin*, Population Reference Bureau, Inc., April, 1976.

Jelliffe, D. B., M.D. "Unique Properties of Human Milk," *The Journal of Reproductive Medicine*, April, 1975.

Lamm, Steven H., and Rosen, John F., M.D. "Lead Contamination in Milks Fed to Infants: 1972–1973," *Pediatrics*, February, 1974.

Margulies, Leah. "Baby Formula Abroad: Exporting Infant Malnutrition," *Christianity and Crisis*, November 10, 1975.

"Mothers Need Mothering," *The Lactation Review*, November 1, 1976.

Nader, Ralph. "Baby Foods: Can You (and Your Baby) Afford Them?," *McCall's*, November, 1970.

Ogberide, M. I., and Goyea, H. Subulola. "The Unfavorable Trend in Infant Feeding," *Environmental Child Health*, February, 1975.

Olney, John W., M.D. "Neurotoxic Effects of Glutamate," *The New England Journal of Medicine,* December 20, 1973.

Olney, John W., M.D., Oi Lan, Ho, M.D., and Vesela, Rhee, M.D. "Brain-Damaging Potential of Protein Hydrolysates," *The New England Journal of Medicine,* August 23, 1973.

Oseid, Betty J., M.D. "Breast-Feeding and Infant Health," *Clinical Obstetrics and Gynecology,* June, 1975.

Rabinowitz, Melba. "Why Didn't Anyone Tell Me About Bottle Mouth Cavities," *Child Today,* March–April, 1974.

Reif-Lehrer, Liane, Ph.D. *The New England Journal of Medicine,* December 4, 1975. This entry appeared in the letters to the editor column.

Reuben, David, M.D. "Dr. David Reuben Answers Your Questions About Breast Feeding," *McCall's,* May, 1971.

Sulzberger, C. L. "Food For More Than Thought," *The New York Times,* February 18, 1976.

"War On Baby Foods," *The Lancet,* April 20, 1974.